HORSE

TRAINING **GUIDE**

Advanced
Western
Riding

by Kara L. Stewart

I-5
PRESS

Advanced Western Riding

Project Team
Roger Sipe, *Special Projects Editor*
Lindsay Hanks, *Associate Editor*
Matt Hennings, *Art Director*
Jessica Jaensch, *Production Coordinator*
Tracy Burns, *Production Coordinator*

I-5 PUBLISHING, LLC
Chief Executive Officer: Mark Harris
Chief Financial Officer: Nicole Fabian
Vice President, Chief Content Officer: June Kikuchi
General Manager, I-5 Press: Christopher Reggio
Editorial Director, I-5 Press: Andrew DePrisco
Art Director, I-5 Press: Mary Ann Kahn
Digital General Manager: Melissa Kauffman
Production Director: Laurie Panaggio
Production Manager: Jessica Jaensch
Marketing Director: Lisa MacDonald

Library of Congress Cataloging-in-Publication Data
Stewart, Kara L.
  Advanced Western riding / by Kara L. Stewart.
    p. cm.
  Horse illustrated training guide.
  Includes bibliographical references and index.
  ISBN 978-1-935484-54-7 (alk. paper)
  1. Western riding. I. Stewart, Kara L. Horse illustrated guide to advanced Western riding. II. Horse illustrated. III. Title.
  SF309.3.S784 2010
  798.2'3--dc22

                 2010021094

This book has been published with the intent to provide accurate and authoritative information in regard to the subject matter within. While every precaution has been taken in the preparation of this book, the author and publisher expressly disclaim any responsibility for any errors, omissions, or adverse effects arising from the use or application of the information contained herein. The techniques and suggestions are used at the reader's discretion and are not to be considered a substitute for veterinary care. If you suspect a medical problem, consult your veterinarian.
The horses in this book are referred to as she and he in alternating chapters unless their sexes are apparent from the activities discussed.

I-5 Publishing, LLC™
3 Burroughs, Irvine, CA 92618
www.facebook.com/i5press
www.i5publishing.com

Printed and bound in China
13 14 15 16 17   1 3 5 7 9 8 6 4 2

dedication

This book is for every rider who seeks a deeper partnership with his or her horse. Stay on the path and follow your heart. The discoveries you make together may astound you.

acknowledgments

*t*hanks Mom and Dad. Your love and support have made everything possible. On our journey through life, the right teachers appear when the student is ready. Each experience leads concretely to the next steps one needs to take.

Thank you, Mark Rashid, Wendy Murdoch, and Andrew Blevins, for being my teachers. Your ideas, integrity, lifelong learning, and gifts for teaching have greatly influenced this book, my horsemanship, and my life.

Mark, thanks for sharing your way of working with horses that transcends horses and applies to all of life. You've helped me see that the knowledge in my head isn't much good until it's part of my soul and that so many wonderful things happen when I bring all of me to my life. I'm a better person because of you. And eternal thanks for introducing me to Aikido.

Wendy, thanks for sharing your brilliant and passionate understanding of human and equine biomechanics. You're helping me and other riders see how everything is possible with the right connections, physical and mental. Thanks for helping me open the door to find presence.

Blevins Sensei, thank you for sharing your talent, time, and passion in your teaching of Aikido and for being a role model in so many ways. Practicing Aikido under your guidance has blessed me and changed my life in more ways than I ever could have imagined.

Deep thanks to Crissi McDonald for your friendship and support and for showing me that stature doesn't matter in working with horses when everything comes from softness; Kathleen Lindley, for your friendship and your insights into so many things; Shannon Brown, for being there in some critical times and sharing your beautiful connection with horses; Wendy Rashid, for all your help over the years; Cherry Hill and Richard Klimesh, for giving me a start and sharing your wisdom; Carole Williams, for being the best mentor ever; Dr. David Siemens, for your perceptive approach to equine anatomy and chiropractic; David Genadek for your ground-breaking ideas in saddle design; the amazing current and past teams at *Horse Illustrated*—Liz Moyer, Holly Werner, Kimberly Abbott, Moira C. Reeve, Karen Keb, and Toni McAllister—for the opportunities and your valuable suggestions over the years; and everyone at BowTie Press who made this a better book.

And thanks to Richard Bangs, Essie Becker, Frances Carbonnel, Peggy Cummings, the Douglas County Writer's Group, Eddie, Joanne Hartmeister, Patricia Hendricks Sensei, Kei and Mariquita Izawa Sensei, John, Sue Littlefield, Mary Mueller, Eva Murphy, Katie Reid, Marion Schneider, James Shaw, Surino, Tasy, Linda Tellington-Jones, Sheila Varian, Suzi Zielinski, and Les-san and John-san and the wonderful students at Kiryu Aikido.

You've all been teachers, role models, guides, and companions on this journey called life. Thanks for sharing this path. I can't wait to see what lies ahead.

Contents

Introduction

Since taking up western riding, you've dedicated yourself to learning more of the details of riding well and improving your riding skills and abilities. No longer a beginner, you're now able to sit confidently at the walk, the jog, and the lope; direct your horse; and influence her speed. But, as you've probably discovered, there is more to being a good rider than just staying in the saddle, steering, and stopping.

Now, you want to be more than a steady passenger; you want to be a partner with your horse. You want to have the type of relationship with your horse that the advanced riders you admire have with their horses. Horse and rider seem to move to the same thoughts, with invisible cues, ease, comfort, and happiness. Talented amateurs and professional trainers make this look easy. For them, riding seems to be a dance. Will you ever ride like that? Can you ever develop such a deep partnership with your horse? The answer is yes! It will take dedication, work, and commitment on your part, but it won't happen overnight. If you persevere and keep the right mind-set, you will reach your goal.

It's helpful, though not essential, to take regular lessons with a trainer who encourages you and keeps raising the bar as you progress. A good trainer can spot areas in which you're struggling, help you work through these issues and push you a little further than you might push yourself if you were riding on your own.

Don't rely on your trainer completely, however. A large part of becoming an advanced western rider is honing your abilities and building your

confidence and knowledge, so one day you will be able to train a horse yourself. As you continue learning, you'll want to develop your own style of horsemanship, one that fits with who you are and is based on the type of partnership you want to have with your horse.

In your quest to become an advanced rider, remember that you can't force the learning process or shorten the length of time it will take to become the rider you seek to be. But you *can* ensure that you keep improving by putting in the saddle time, not taking shortcuts, getting strong in the basics, and continuing to refine what you know.

Although there is no substitute for hard, dedicated work, there is one more critical aspect to becoming an advanced rider: your mind-set. At a certain point, you may find that riding becomes less about cues and technique and more about mentally connecting with your horse, riding with her rather than simply on her.

In this book, we'll explore some ideas that will help you refine your riding and open the door to a lifetime of improving your skills. The only limitations are your confidence in yourself and the goals you set for yourself and your horse. First, we'll look at some of the mental aspects of riding that set advanced riders apart; then we'll discuss ways to refine your riding by developing better balance, aids, and timing, as well as cover areas you may not be as familiar with, such as your breathing, intent, and focus.

Then, we'll explore advanced work such as self-carriage in you and your horse, collection, transitions, and lateral movement. You'll also learn more about tack and the importance of correct saddle fit. And you will get tips for preparing for various types of competitions, from horse shows to cattle work. Finally, you will learn about other ways to have fun with your equine partner.

So ride all you can and practice seriously but joyfully! Riding is a gift, and it's meant to be fun. Keep smiling, no matter what and, above all, enjoy the journey.

Working with a trainer can help you progress, but you should also develop your own horsemanship skills.

CHAPTER 1

Moving Beyond the Basics

*t*he best riders never stop learning or seeking new ways to do things. They continually strive to refine what they know, ask with less pressure, and get in better timing with their horses.

As you advance in your horsemanship, you, too, will find truth in the saying, "The more you know, the more you realize there is to learn."

This ongoing challenge of discovery, to deepen your understanding of horses and learn how best to work with them, will help you reach the levels of horsemanship skill you seek to attain. These layers of knowledge are what keep expert riders progressing and learning—and loving every minute in the saddle. As you become more advanced, you'll discover that good riding is as much (if not more) about mental creativity and control as it is about pure physical technique. In fact, the most successful riders may simply be better than the average rider at harnessing these mental aspects of riding.

This chapter offers some topics to get you thinking about the mental side of riding that will be helpful in advancing your skills. But don't stop here. Use these ideas as a springboard to see what else you can come up with.

Keep Riding; Stay in the Moment

If you're driving a car and it starts to skid on a slippery curve, do you immediately throw open the door and bail out? Not likely! Unfortunately, bailing out—physically or mentally—is exactly how some riders react when their horses do something unexpected. In a split second, such riders relinquish their influence on the outcome of the situation.

For example, your horse might spook at a dog and then stop. If you are caught off guard by the spook, you might be left behind and end up on the ground. But if you stay relaxed and remain physically and mentally connected to your horse during the spook, which will be over in a second or two, your horse is likely to quickly regain his composure because you haven't lost yours.

Keep riding through every situation. In other words: Don't bail out—literally or figuratively. When you only have a few seconds of reaction time, don't decide you're going to fall off and start looking for the best place to land. Instead, try to safely help your horse through the situation. (Of course, there are times when dismounting is the best idea, but try to do it as a planned event rather than as an action taken in panic.)

In addition to maintaining your commitment to continue riding—mentally and physically—no matter what happens, it's important to stay in the moment. However, there's a fine line between staying in the moment and creating self-fulfilling prophecies of negative outcomes. Every time you ride, work toward the goal of riding with enough awareness to anticipate a problem and to be able to defuse or avoid it. Do not mentally jump ahead to the worst possible outcome. Unfortunately, this is exactly what some riders do, and they bring it about by expecting the worst to occur. Knowing there is always a loose dog at the blue house up ahead on the left, for example, the rider tenses up, certain the dog

will come running out and the horse will spook. Feeling his rider tense up, the horse obliges with an enthusiastic spook and bolts down the road!

Instead, strive to ride every step; don't project too far into the future. Horses are creatures of the here and now, and the best riders help their horses every moment. This isn't accomplished by micromanaging his every move but rather by staying aware and directing him before he has the chance to take his thought completely away from you.

Staying in the moment will also help if you decide to compete with your horse. Whether in reining, western pleasure, or a cow class, if you make a mistake, you can't go back and fix it. It will only hinder your performance if you dwell on the mistake. However, if you stay in the moment, you can continue to ride every step from there on and make the rest of your ride as good as it can be.

Leave Out the Emotions; Assume the Best

Have you ever watched someone severely reprimand a horse for a transgression and thought that the rider or handler actually enjoyed getting angry and correcting his or her horse? This is the behavior of an amateur, and it shouldn't be emulated or admired.

Advanced horse riders are able to separate their emotions from their corrections. They can make corrections without anger, embarrassment, frustration, or other negative emotions. It is done in a matter-of-fact "I'm looking for this, not that" sort of mind-set, with the intention of helping the horse understand rather than forcing him to comply.

When you need to correct your horse, think of it in the same way as correcting a child, which you would do calmly, considerately, and clearly,

If you make a mistake, don't dwell on it. Do what this rider is doing: Move on and make the rest of your ride as good as it can be.

Here, a rider makes corrections in a helpful, matter-of-fact way, rather than letting her emotions get the best of her.

instead of with escalating anger, a raised voice, and pumping adrenaline. Taking emotions out of corrections can go a long way in training. Your horse stays in a willing mind set, ready to try what you ask, and you are able to evaluate what he is offering and reward him for his efforts.

You may have noticed that you'd rather spend time with people who assume the best rather than those who assume the worst and with those who have positive outlooks rather than those who whine and complain. Wouldn't our horses appreciate this, too?

The next time you're at the barn, listen to what other riders say and how they say it. How many of them compile long lists of what their horses are doing wrong (and how it's usually the horses' faults) and complain about how this or that trick or behavior could be better? You might be surprised at how negative the comments can get!

The power of positive thinking is a proven approach to many areas of life, so why not apply it to your horsemanship? Instead of looking for everything that's wrong or bad, start looking for the good that you and your horse are doing, then build on that. Often, the more you concentrate on the good and the less energy you spend on the bad, the more likely it is that, over time, the good outweighs the not-so-good. After a while, you may even look back and realize that the problems you used to have are now gone.

Perhaps you can't do a perfect walk-lope departure yet. That's OK. Do the jog-lope transition you're really good at and occasionally try a walk-lope transition. If it's not perfect, don't make a big deal out of it; just keep going. Over time, it's highly likely that you will eventually find yourself doing a pretty good departure because you didn't make such a fuss over the less-than-perfect one.

If your horse isn't doing what you think you're asking, treat him like a friend and assume the best rather than the worst. Assume he doesn't understand or is confused. Perhaps he's not able to do what you're asking because he's not physically developed or coordinated enough yet. Or he may be trying to tell you that he's in pain. Doesn't considering this perspective of what's happening different from the automatic assumption that he's being disobedient, willful,

Instead of dwelling on the negatives, this rider is focusing on what her horse is doing well.

or resistant? He may be avoiding doing what you ask but with good reason, according to his thought process.

If your horse doesn't do what you ask, also take a look at how you're asking. Break the request down into smaller pieces and see if this works.

There are no limits to the ways in which you can improve as you seek to advance your skills and those of your horse. To do so, it helps to reframe the areas needing improvement, not as bad or negative behaviors but simply as areas you need to work on together.

Be Consistent

Many cartoons have depicted horses plotting ways to make us angry, to embarrass us in front of friends, or to make us look incompetent in front of judges. In reality, a horse's actions usually are not directed toward the rider. He is merely doing what he has found to be correct in similar situations, based on your teachings

(or someone else's). Or he is doing what he thinks is going to help him at that moment.

Your horse's actions may be the result of miscommunication. Something he considers correct behavior but which you don't—such as dragging you along to get to a few sprigs of grass—may be behavior you have inadvertently created and rewarded by inconsistently responding whenever he offered this behavior in the past. We are training our horses every moment we are with them. We just may not be teaching them the behaviors we think we are.

It's consistency—having the same expectations and rules every day, all of the time, no matter what—that helps our horses to learn what's expected of them and to behave the way we would like them. Being consistent with our horses sounds simple and obvious, doesn't it? However, it's all too easy to let our consistency waver. Just imagine yourself in the following scenario and see if you find any similarities to your daily interactions with your horse:

Consider this scenario: As you lead your horse in from the pasture, he crowds you and

This horse is just being a horse—snatching some grass. His actions aren't meant to personally irritate the rider.

even scoots ahead, making circles around you. Your mind may be on your upcoming lesson, so you just get out of his way, and the two of you keep up this circular dance all the way to the barn. The next day, you bring your horse in as usual. However, on this day, you are upset. Perhaps your boss blamed you for something that wasn't your fault, and you're still steaming about it. Your horse acts exactly as he did the day before: He crowds you, scoots ahead, and makes a circle. This time, you are having none of it. You slap him on the chest and yank his lead rope. After all, he *should* know better than to do this.

Who's being inconsistent here? Your horse is just doing what you allowed on the day before; you taught him that it was acceptable. Then, twenty-four hours later, you changed the rules, but he didn't know that. He's not likely leading this way to be naughty; you haven't set consistent standards and maintained the parameters whenever you're together—all of the time, no matter what.

Horses are steady creatures, and they thrive on positive consistency. If you are consistent with your horse day in and day out, he'll know what to expect and what is allowed and not allowed. Because of your consistency and level-headedness, your horse will start seeing you as a leader he can put his trust in. You may be able to get his attention by smacking him, but, at that point, you've stopped being a leader and are just reacting to a behavior.

What should you do if your horse has a behavior that you know you've helped create but now want to get rid of? Isn't this also changing the rules and being inconsistent? Won't it be confusing or disconcerting to your horse, even upsetting to him?

This is a good observation. You have horses because you enjoy being around them, and you want them to enjoy being around you. There's nothing wrong with this; the mutual enjoyment of each other's company is a good mind-set to cultivate. Problems can arise when you interact with your horse based on whether he will like you.

For example: You may feed him treats and allow him to overeagerly snuffle your pockets, which leads to nipping. Or perhaps you don't consistently ask him to give you a certain amount of space, which leads to him inadvertently running into you. Over time, your horse may see the pocket searching and crowding behaviors as acceptable, and perhaps even wanted, because you are not indicating otherwise. If you try to correct these behaviors, your horse may very well act a little put out and unhappy with you and your new rules.

Keep your rules fair and considerate, be consistent and calm when enforcing them, and don't second-guess yourself. Before long, your horse will accept the new rules and be fine with them. Your horse will like you and will be happy to see you when you have proven to him that you are fair, consistent, levelheaded, matter-of-fact, and appreciative of his efforts.

Feel Free to Make Mistakes

Even professional trainers make mistakes with their horses from time to time; they just tend to make fewer mistakes simply because they have more experience. Over time, you also will develop the feel, timing, and awareness to know when to quit for the day, when to press for just a little more effort, and when to switch to another task.

Let's say you've been working on walk-lope transitions, and you just nailed one. Your horse is round, soft, happy, and carrying himself well in a balanced lope. You're grinning at how great the transition was—no swishing tail, no cranky ears. Your horse just collected himself and stepped into the lope without any hesitation.

Even though there's a little voice inside you telling you to end the day on that perfect note, you ignore it. The transition was so perfect, you want to do it again and be sure it wasn't a fluke. You bring your horse back down to a walk, wait

a few strides, then cue again for the lope. This time, he swishes his tail, raises his head, and takes two strides of jog before loping.

Well, you think you can't end on that sour note, so you regroup and try again. This time it's even worse. Now your horse is tight and a little crabby, and you're really angry at yourself for pushing him through this and negating the perfect transition he gave you ten minutes ago.

This is a perfect example of the consequences of making a poor decision. Would it have been better if you'd simply quit for the day after the flawless transition? To be honest: Yes, that would have been the best decision.

However, living in the past and regretting your actions doesn't help you or your horse. The good news is that horses are pretty resilient and forgiving of honest mistakes. When you make a mistake,

Be fair and considerate when you interact with your horse, and he will be happy to see you.

Horses without a confident, decisive rider may demonstrate unwanted behaviors such as rearing, as shown here, out of a feeling of insecurity.

move on and be gentle to yourself and your horse. Embrace your mistakes and learn from them, but try your best not to repeat them in the future!

If you're working with your horse and nothing seems to be going right or your work is taking a downward spiral, stop and take a deep breath. You may want to dismount and take a break. You can even just call it quits for the day. There's no harm in starting over again the next day with a calm, fresh mind. In fact, this approach can help you get to your goal faster than if you were to push through and cause a fight.

You may have heard that you have to win every time you're with your horse and that he must always do what you're asking. You also may have heard that he will learn to take advantage of you if you quit before he complies. Actually, you'll have more ground to make up if you lose your temper and push through an issue or if you frighten your horse and cause him to lose confidence in you. Then you'll have to go back, fix these issues, and regain lost trust later.

It's better to approach training at your horse's pace. Slow down when you feel he's getting confused or frustrated. By working calmly through an issue, you will figure it out in a way that makes sense to you and your horse.

It can also be helpful to remember that, as with any long-term endeavor, your progress in riding may sometimes feel as if you take two steps forward and one step back. That's OK; you're still making progress! Take heart that the learning process isn't always a straight trajectory. In fact, learning is often taking place during the difficult phases; you just can't see it yet.

Be Confident and Decisive

Generally speaking, you'll be fine if you are confident that what you're asking of your horse is within reason and within his capabilities, that you are acting with your horse's best interests in mind, and that you and your horse will be OK.

Problems can arise when you start doubting yourself and not following through on decisions. You may also become so paralyzed at the fear of doing something wrong that you end up doing nothing at all. These two scenarios can result in undesirable behaviors from your horse.

If you provide no direction or you waffle about what you're asking for, your horse might react to your lack of confidence in a variety of ways. He may start making the decisions because he feels safer doing so. He may react explosively to small concerns because he's not confident you can help him. He may stop doing anything you ask because you lack conviction and he's not going to do all the work himself. These are just a few of the results that can stem from your lack of confidence or direction.

So make a decision and act on it. If it doesn't work out the way you wanted, you can always try something different. The important thing is to have confidence in your decision and to move forward.

Practice Being the Person You Want to Be

Who you are in the saddle is the same as who you are out of the saddle. For example, if you spend your day feeling harried and stressed from working at a demanding job and sitting hunched in front of a computer, and if you are unfocused with your family and aggressive toward other drivers on the commute, you'll bring at least some of these traits with you when you work with your horse. It's just not possible to flip a switch and become a calm, considerate, patient, thinking person when you go to the barn and saddle up if you don't practice these traits in the other hours of your day.

If you tend to be angry and uptight, practice being more considerate and understanding of the people (and animals) around you. If you tend to finish other people's sentences and rush to conclusions, practice being quiet and listening. If you tend to be aggressive, practice being just assertive instead. And if you tend to be passive, practice being a little more assertive. The end result will be well worth it.

Have Fun

It's a fair guess that you got into the horse hobby because you thought it would be fun. Whether your goals were trail riding, showing, or cattle work, the thought of spending time with a good horse made you happy.

As you become more advanced and seek to continually improve your skills or even start competing, you may find, surprisingly, that you're having less fun. This may be because you've set higher goals or because you expect more from yourself and your horse than you did in the past.

Goals and expectations are good things, but it may be time to take a step back if you find yourself becoming overly serious and not having as much fun as you used to. Sometimes, when things don't seem to go right, it may mean that you're trying too hard. And if you're not having much fun, chances are that your horse isn't having a great time, either!

Try backing off a little. Just spend time enjoying your horse. Go for a trail ride. Treat him to a great grooming session. Forget your agenda and goals for a few days, and see if you can't regain the joy you felt when you first started riding.

You may find that, when you keep your dedication to improvement but let go of the all-or-nothing approach, you actually progress further and more quickly because the unnecessary pressure is gone. Go ride and smile! There's no better way to spend time than with your horse.

CHAPTER 2

Refine Your Riding

*a*dvanced western riding isn't about strength, grip, and force. It's about allowing movement, influencing it without blocking it, and directing that movement and energy into the outcome you want.

You can attain this by improving your balance, seat, aids, and cues. In addition, the more you can refine your timing, breathing, focus, awareness, and other subtle aspects of riding, the deeper the partnership you can build with your horse.

Here are a few areas to explore that will help you increase your riding skills as you continue to advance.

Developing Better Balance and Seat

When you boil it down to its simplest elements, good western riding is about sitting on your horse in a softly supported way, with your skeleton correctly aligned so your bones, instead of your muscles, can do the work of supporting you.

You're secure in the saddle and not gripping with your legs or using your hands for balance. This frees you to give aids independently and to use only the pressure necessary to get a response.

But every rider has certain body idiosyncrasies and habits that can make riding correctly more difficult than it needs to be. Once you become aware of how you move, hold yourself, and use your body, you can start changing patterns for the better.

The postures and body habits you have in your daily life definitely affect how you ride your horse. You are what you practice. If, for example, most of your days are spent in front of a computer, with rounded shoulders and a collapsed back, it will be difficult to ride with good posture when you get on your horse.

Your breathing patterns also affect your riding. If you normally breathe shallowly and into your upper chest, it will be difficult to switch to

the low, deep, rhythmic breathing conducive to good riding. (We'll cover breathing in more detail at the end of this chapter.)

Imagine the effect your head (which weighs about ten pounds—about the same as a bowling ball) has on your posture if it's not carried in an efficient position so your skeleton can support it. If your neck and shoulder muscles have to carry this weight around all day, that's a recipe for pain and poor posture in the saddle.

It's also important to realize that horses often mirror their riders; if a rider has a hollow back, the horse will typically travel with a hollow back as well. Generous creatures that they are, horses often compensate for our imbalances. The more balanced and symmetrical we can be, the better our horses can move. Learning to feel your horse's rhythm in different gaits can also help you refine your seat and balance.

The good news is that, even if you're only able to ride a few hours a week, you can practice the posture, alignment, and breathing that you want to bring to your riding during the many hours of your days that you're not riding.

The first step to developing better balance and a more secure seat is to become aware of your natural patterns and habits. Then, you can work toward letting go of unnecessary muscle tension and play with finding the position that is most secure for you. Here are some suggestions to get you started.

WORK WITH WHAT YOU HAVE

No one has perfect symmetry, alignment, or posture; just like your horse, you have physical issues and quirks. You can, however, work around them and overcome them with awareness and education.

Over a period of a week or two, pay attention to your body movements: Notice how you walk, stand, sit, move, and breathe. (Don't make judgments about what is right and wrong; just become aware of what is normal for you.) Start noticing other people's postures and habits, too. It can be an educational experience.

Do you tend to arch your lower back or round your upper back? Where are your shoulders in relation to your hips? Do you walk with your chest leading, your hips leading, or something in between? Do you walk with your head tilted to one side? Do you regularly stand with more weight on one hip than the other? How do you breathe—low, high, deep, shallow? Does your breathing change depending on how much stress you're under?

Often, these habits are so ingrained that it can be difficult to identify them, and they certainly feel correct because it's how you're used to moving and breathing every minute of your day.

All of your habits in your daily life will carry over to your riding. If you notice asymmetries, it can be very helpful to seek the services of a good body worker who specializes in body alignment, such as a Feldenkrais or Alexander Technique practitioner, a chiropractor, a physical therapist, a massage therapist, and so on. A professional may be able to help you reeducate your body and nervous system so you can start carrying your body more efficiently. Eventually, you won't have to think about moving differently on your horse because the new behaviors will become natural for you.

LET GO OF THE BRACES

The more advanced you become as a rider, the more important it will be to ride with softness, in balance, and giving subtle cues. Becoming aware of your braces—and then letting them go—will help you progress toward this goal. But what is a brace? A brace is any extra muscle power, extra energy, or extra motion used to accomplish a certain task. Let's use vacuuming as an example.

The next time you're cleaning a carpet with an upright vacuum, notice what your body does as you pull and push the vacuum over the carpet. When you pull the vacuum back, are you simply swinging your elbow back from your shoulder joint, without raising your arm? Or are you putting in more effort than you need? Are you hiking your shoulder up and back in a circular motion as you pull the vacuum toward you? Are you swinging your whole torso around as you pull the vacuum back? Vacuuming this way uses a lot of unnecessary muscle power. These are braces. Many people develop habits that use more muscle power and energy than is really necessary to complete tasks. Over time, these habits can lead to injury or chronic pain.

To eliminate your braces, start by being aware of them. For example, when you're driving or sitting at work, be aware of what you do. Notice whether you grip the steering wheel more tightly or hold the mouse with more force than is necessary. Try seeing how little effort you can use to do all the daily tasks in your life.

Use this same awareness to your horse. When you get on your horse, take a moment to scan your body, head to toe, for braces. If you become aware of one, try to let it go. In doing so, be careful that you don't tense up one area to release another! Make everything easy and comfortable, and have fun with it. You can't pass or fail. This process, both on and off your horse, really does last a lifetime.

See whether you ride better when you release your brace, and notice how your horse responds. Try walking your horse while you are relaxed, then brace and tighten one leg, one arm, one hand, or one finger. See what happens. Does she slow down or speed up, flick her ears back and forth, clench her jaw, or swish her tail? Again, there are no right or wrong answers at this point; you're just becoming aware of how everything you do affects your horse.

FIND YOUR MOST SECURE POSITION

Through her years studying biomechanics and correct body alignment, riding instructor Sally Swift pioneered a new approach to riding that she called "centered riding." When St. Martin's Press published her book by the same name in 1985, it revolutionized riding instruction and helped riders find the position that is correct and most stable for their bodies. Wendy Murdoch, a long-time student of Swift, took these ideas to an even higher level in her work. She shares her findings with riders around the world and in her book *Simplify Your Riding* (Carriage House Publishing, 2004). Other instructors and trainers (such as Peggy Cummings, Mark Rashid, and Dr. Deb Bennett) have also studied biomechanics and how a rider's position in the saddle helps or hinders the horse.

Riding from a correct position means that your body is aligned so you don't have to rely on extra muscle power to keep you safely upright on your horse. Not surprisingly, a correct position relates directly to a stable and secure position.

In the saddle, this means all parts of your body are properly aligned. Your ear, elbow, hip, and heel are vertically aligned. Your seat bones are pointed straight down, and your pelvis is in

Do you walk with your head down or take longer strides with one leg? Bring awareness to how you use your body and notice how others use theirs.

A rider braces against his horse's movement. Bracing is using more muscle, energy, or motion than necessary, and it can lead to discomfort and pain for horse and rider.

a neutral position. Your back is soft and supported, somewhere between an arched, hollowed position and a rounded, collapsed position. Your breathing expands your lower rib cage and belly rather than lifting your chest. This position doesn't change drastically from one style of riding to another.

When you are sitting in the saddle in the position that is most stable for your conformation, your body is free to move in any direction to match the movement of your horse. You can influence her movement and speed because your aids are independent of each other. Because you aren't relying on grip or using unnecessary muscle power, you can use your aids to softly and effectively influence your horse.

To find the position that is best for you, start by sitting on the edge of a hard chair. This allows you to feel your seat bones. Locate the top of your pelvis by putting your hands at the sides of your waist, then moving them down until you feel bone. Play with how rotating your pelvis affects the position of your seat bones.

While on the chair, sit the way you normally ride. Notice whether your back is hollowed (the top of your pelvis is rotated forward) or whether your back is rounded (the top of your pelvis is rotated backward). Every rider will have a different position in which his or her body is the most balanced and stable. Play with rotating your pelvis—first with rather exaggerated movements, then with smaller and smaller movements. Find the place where your pelvis is softly centered between an arched back and a hollowed back, and try to remember how this feels.

Next, take your experiment to your horse. How do changes in your position affect her? Start at the walk. Does she go faster? Slower? Stop altogether?

If you have trouble finding the position that is most secure for your body type and individual characteristics, seek out the educated eyes of a trainer or expert who's acutely attuned to body position and the biomechanics behind it. This person will help you learn to refine your position based on what's mechanically correct

This rider relaxes his foot outside the stirrup. As you ride, scan your body for any braces and release them.

rather than on what is popular in the show pen or is used in a certain discipline at the moment.

Frequently, an additional benefit of learning to ride correctly from a strong and stable position is a reduction of pain. Riding in good alignment, without excess muscular exertion, can make a big difference in your comfort and future riding enjoyment.

Keep in mind, too, that your saddle will have an effect on your position. If you continually struggle with keeping your legs underneath you or if you always feel that you're being left behind the motion of your horse, it very well could be because of the geometry of your saddle. (See Chapter 4 for more about basic saddle fitting for performance.)

To test whether you have attained your own position of balance and stability, ask for a friend's help and mount up. Hold a rein in each hand and have your friend stand on the ground

Have a friend check your saddle position if necessary.

just in front of your horse. Sit and breathe as you normally do. Then ask your friend to hold the reins about six inches from the bit and apply steady pressure to the reins in a straight line from your hands toward the bit, not up or down. If your alignment and breathing are correct, your friend's pressure on the reins will only pull you deeper into the saddle. If you're not sitting correctly (with a good alignment of your head, elbow, hip, and heel and with your breathing correct), your friend will easily pull you up and out of the saddle!

If this is what happens, play around with adjusting your pelvis slightly in one direction and then in the other, to see whether this prevents you from being pulled out of the saddle when your friend pulls on the reins. Try altering your arm position, as well, to see how this changes your secure position. Try changing your breathing from high in your chest to lower in your ribs. Does this change the outcome?

Once you find a solid position, be aware of it, and try to replicate it every time you ride. Have your friend test you now and then to see whether you are maintaining your most stable position.

FEEL THE RHYTHM

Another way to develop better balance and seat is to start thinking in terms of rhythm and beat while riding. Horses are rhythmic creatures, and they seem to appreciate it when we do things using a steady flow, such as grooming them with a steady rhythm of brush strokes and breathing with steady inhales and exhales instead of holding our breath while we're with them.

You can take this a step further by riding as if you have a metronome under your saddle horn (there actually are metronomes made for riders) or have a song in your head that has a certain tempo for different gaits. If you are able to play music in your arena, try riding to songs with good, steady beats and see how enjoyable it can be for you and your horse.

To ride to a certain beat, first get in time with your horse's gait. The walk has four beats; the jog, two; and the lope, three. Don't drive with your seat to increase your horse's speed, which actually makes many horses slow down or stop because the pressure puts their weight on their forehand. Don't squeeze or kick harder with your legs. Instead, try changing the tempo. For example, if you want to increase the speed of the walk, increase the tempo of the four-beat rhythm in your head. It's not an obvious change or force of movement; however, it allows your body to move to the new tempo.

As you're doing this, keep your hips and knees relaxed because gripping and tightening will just restrict your horse's movement. Sure, horses can and do learn to move well, even when their riders hinder their natural flowing movement, but it's easier when you can help facilitate rather than hinder their movements.

You can also use rhythm and beat to change gaits through upward and downward transitions. Try picking up a nice flowing walk. Notice the definite four-beat movement and count the beat aloud or silently. If your body is soft and not braced in any of your joints, your hips will rotate in a sort of figure-eight pattern: up, forward, down, and back in time with the horse's walk. Notice that each of your hips moves independently to follow the two halves of your horse's back, which also move independently.

Now, to transition to a nice jog, change the four-beat rhythm into two beats in your head, and allow your body to pick up this beat. Horses are so sensitive that they often will change their gait to match your new rhythm. Try it and see. If you don't get the change of gait to the jog, add a little leg and be sure to release your leg as soon as you feel the increase in energy. Then play with changing your internal beat from two to three beats to ask for a lope.

Your horse may not immediately change gaits when you change the tempo in your head and in your body; but the more aware you are of rhythm and beat, the more you can use it to become a better rider and a more effective partner with your horse.

Try changing gaits by changing the rhythm in your head. Here a horse and rider transition from a walk to a jog.

TAKE A LAP ON THE LONGE

One proven way to enhance your balance and seat is to take advantage of lessons on the longe (or lunge) line. Riding on the longe is not just for beginners, so take longe-line lessons whenever you can. Even the most advanced riders spend time on the longe line to improve their abilities.

While your trainer sends your horse out in a circle, you are free to concentrate on how it feels to move with your horse at different gaits and maintain balance and stability while in motion. Without the need for reins to steer or slow your horse, you'll also discover whether you're relying on the reins for balance. If you are, this can come as a big surprise, especially if you didn't previously believe that you were.

During your longe lessons, focus on keeping your breathing rhythmic and in time with the gait, and breathe into your ribs rather than your chest. See how many strides you get with a single inhale, then a single exhale, and play with increasing this interval.

Feel how your horse's back moves at each gait. The walk may feel like a figure eight, flowing sideways and forward and back in a continuous movement. Be aware of the movement but don't try to emphasize any one direction over another.

The jog may feel primarily up and down in movement, especially if your horse's jog isn't very smooth. A little forward-and-around movement will occur, too. To sit the jog softly, you need to allow your pelvis and hips to match these movements.

At the lope, you may feel a swoop of energy underneath you as the horse is suspended in midair for a split second before her outside hind foot lands. You'll also feel a very small reach with your hip that corresponds to the lead your horse is on. If your horse is on the left lead, you'll feel this reaching with your left hip.

While on the longe, try some stretching exercises and anything else you and your trainer can think of to develop a more secure seat. Your goal is to ride well using good balance and alignment rather than bracing, holding with the reins, or being put into position by your saddle. For an even greater challenge, try riding without stirrups, then using only a bareback pad.

Refining Effective Aids and Cues

As you become more advanced in your riding, you'll want to start refining your aids and cues so that everything will be invisible to an onlooker. This is the goal to strive for. If you keep working toward this, you'll look back a year from now and see how much more subtle and refined you've become as a rider. One of the fun things about refining your aids and cues is that it can lead to a lifetime of further exploration and refinement. You can take it as far as you want.

Even though there may be a well-known approach to cuing for a particular movement—and it's fine to start with the conventional cue—play with refining it even further. Keep in mind also that horses don't read training books. If a traditional cue just isn't working for your horse, try something different and see what happens.

As you start to refine your cues and aids, it's helpful to know what you're looking for, to start at the lowest amount of pressure and release at the correct time, and to vow to never get into a pulling match (or a fight) with your horse.

KNOW WHAT RESPONSE YOU EXPECT
Clarity in horse training is very important. After all, if you don't know exactly what you're asking for, how can you reward your horse promptly for responding correctly? If, for example, you're asking your horse to back up, what are your specific expectations? If she is just learning to

back up, are you only looking for her to submit to the pressure of the bit, perhaps to drop her head a fraction of an inch or to shift her weight backward? Or is she a well-trained horse that can give you a few steps backward? What you ask for depends on your horse's level of training and how much prior knowledge she has.

Knowing what response you expect before you ask your horse to do something allows you to reward your horse when she gets it right or to keep asking if you don't quite get the response you expect.

YOUR PRESSURE SCALE
One very important idea to help you advance your riding skills is to use as little pressure as possible but as much as is necessary to get the change you're looking for. Doing too little—and getting no response from your horse—doesn't necessarily make you a soft rider, but it can make you an ineffective rider.

To get the response you're looking for when you begin training, you may need to use more pressure than you'd like to for a period of time. If your horse needs more pressure to understand your request initially, that's OK. Just remember to always begin with the cue you ultimately want to use. This will help your horse become as soft and responsive to cues as possible.

This approach will take you far in your western riding. It will ensure that you can ride any horse and work well with her because you are adapting your riding to each horse's needs rather than keeping your skills static.

Let's say you're asking your horse to pick up a jog from a walk. Start with a nice free-flowing walk, then choose a place to start jogging. It can be the far corner of the arena, a tree down the trail, or any other place that you want. Choosing a concrete location for your transition will allow you to focus, organize your thoughts, and direct your energy. As you near the chosen place, think "jog" and see what happens. If your horse doesn't respond, squeeze with your legs using light pressure. Even if she simply gets a little more energy, that's great. At first, you're looking for a change and an increase in energy, not necessarily the full transition from walk to jog. Remember to release your legs the instant she responds with a little more energy. This release of pressure lets your horse know she's done something correctly.

If your horse doesn't respond to the small cue, don't ignore her lack of response. Doing so won't help her become softer to your aids. At this stage, although soft leg pressure may be all the pressure and cue you want to use, you may need to use a slightly bigger cue initially to get the change you are looking for.

Remember to ask with the cue you ultimately want to use first and wait for a response. If you don't get the response, increase the pressure to the point where your horse understands what you want. If you're riding a very sensitive horse, increasing the pressure may mean just adding a kissing or clucking noise. A less sensitive horse may need a decisive tap with a crop, just once, immediately after your cue. The next time you

ask for a jog, start again with the small squeeze of your leg that you want to use as the cue and see whether she responds this time by stepping up into the jog.

You may find it helpful to rate increasing pressure on a scale from 1 to 10. The 1 on your scale may be the bare minimum of cues (such as the mere thought of asking for a jog), and the 10 on your scale would be more pressure than you'd ever use (chasing her with a tractor). Your 1 and 10 levels of pressure will vary depending on your current skill level, and it's fun to see how you can change the parameters of your levels of pressure over time as you and your horse become a better team. Today, your 1 may be a squeeze with your legs, and your 10 may be a tap from a crop. In a few years, your 1 might be refined to a weight shift, and your 10 might be a squeeze with your legs. Make this a game of seeing how little it takes to ask your horse to do something. When your 10 becomes your 1, then redefine your parameters!

Use only as much pressure or cue as your horse needs. Otherwise she may resent your "shouting," communicated here by tail swishing and ear flicking.

RELEASING CUES

Horses learn by trial and error, just as we do. After all, a horse is not born with the knowledge that the pressure of a leg aid means "please move over" or that the rein on her neck means "please turn the opposite way." Horses have to learn that "cue A equals response B" by trying different answers to the questions you ask and discovering what the results are.

Especially when you're working with your horse on something new, remember to release your cue (the pressure) the instant she even thinks about offering what you're looking for and tries to do what you've asked. It's the release of pressure that lets your horse know she's on the right track, so it's important to stop cuing when she's trying.

If you're teaching your horse to side-pass, for example, release the pressure as she shifts her weight to the side. Don't keep the pressure on expecting an entire step, or she may get frustrated because she doesn't yet know that this particular cue means to move her body sideways. Build on the weight shift. Next, reward her for lifting a foot, then for moving an entire leg, then for taking a step. Rewarding these small attempts will let your horse know she's on the right track and is giving the answers you're looking for.

To notice these tiny attempts, you must be quiet enough in your body and your mind. It may be tempting to get louder with bigger cues if nothing is happening, but you may miss what your horse is offering. If you miss her response the first time, she may decide she got the answer wrong and avoid trying that movement again.

PULLING MATCHES ARE FOR TRACTORS

If you miss your horse's attempts because you're too loud or hasty in your cues or because you're not quiet enough to feel a change, you may inadvertently start a pulling contest. Horses outweigh humans by several hundred pounds, and they'll always have the advantage in sheer strength. If you ever feel that you're getting into a pulling match with your horse, change tactics. She won't pull by herself if she doesn't have anything to pull against.

Instead of pulling, release pressure just as your horse starts doing what you ask.

Let's say you're asking your horse to back up. Slow down mentally and physically. Ask for a shift of weight to the rear and reward it if she complies. If you don't get a response, lifting just one rein instead of pulling harder on both reins. Otherwise, your horse may meet your pull on both reins and add to it. Or try tilting her head to the side to break the hind end free, then build on that movement. Move on to another task, take a break, or do anything else that is productive rather than giving in to the temptation to start pulling.

And above all, resist turning a pulling match into a full-blown fight. Neither of you will win, even if you succeed in making your horse do what you demanded.

Timing Cues for Greatest Effectiveness

As you've already read, horses' gaits consist of certain beats and rhythms that are created by the pattern of each hoof landing on the ground in a particular order. While a foot is in the air, its direction can be influenced. When a foot is on the ground or nearly on the ground, it is committed to that path, and you have to wait until the next stride to influence it. You can learn to time your cues to coincide with the moment when it is easiest for your horse to respond to your request. Learning the basics of footfall patterns in each gait and correct cue timing can help your horse respond quickly and easily to your requests.

Although it may sound daunting to learn which foot is doing what, it's really not that difficult to master. It's all about biomechanics and how the skeleton (whether yours or your horse's) moves through space and follows the laws of gravity. For example, the next time you go for a walk, notice that, when your right foot is completely on the ground, your left heel has lifted off the ground and your left toes are about to follow. Your horse moves in similarly predictable ways, all based on anatomy and physics. When you can start feeling where your horse's feet are, you can start using your cues more effectively.

FOOTFALL BASICS

One way to determine how a horse's feet move in relation to her body is to watch (and feel while you're riding) the swing of her barrel. In general terms, the horse's barrel must move out of the way so there is room for her legs to come underneath her. How much and in what direction the barrel moves depends on the gait and the degree of collection, as well as on the horse's conformation and breeding. However, every horse moves in the same general way when walking, jogging, and loping. Gaited horses move with different patterns of footfall, but the basics of movement still apply.

Take turns with your friends walking your horses in straight lines so you can see how the barrel moves and how each foot moves in relation with the barrel movement. Then, put a horse on the longe line, and study the movement of the horse and her footfall patterns at a jog and a lope. Here's a quick look at gait analysis, as well as some tips to keep in mind as you refine your understanding of a horse's movement.

Walk

The walk is a four-beat gait in which a horse's feet move hind, front on one side, then hind, front on the other side. This means she will step left hind, left front, right hind, right front.

The horse's barrel will swing out and back in, to allow her legs to come underneath her body. So when the barrel nears the apex of its swing to the right, the right hind will be coming off the ground. When the barrel swings past the midline and starts out toward the left, the right front will be coming off the ground. When the barrel continues to the apex of swing on the left side, the left hind is coming off the ground, and when the barrel continues back right past the midline, the left front is coming off the ground.

To feel this swinging when you're riding, become aware of how your legs and your pelvis move in time with the horse's barrel. Can you feel the side-to-side swing of your horse's barrel? If you can't, see if you can identify any braces and let them go. Now can you feel the swing? You may feel this movement more in your hip joint or in your shoulder than in your lower leg or thigh. Every rider is different, so there's no specific area

The horse's direction and speed can be influenced at the moment when the horse's foot is coming off the ground.

of your body where you are supposed to feel the movement; just soften and try to feel it. But don't emphasize the movement in your pelvis or try to force your seat to move with your horse's movement. Again, just become aware of it.

Jog

The jog is a two-beat diagonal gait, so the right front and left hind legs move together as a pair, and the left front and right hind legs move together. There is also a barrel swing associated with the jog, but it is much more subtle than the swing at the walk.

Can you feel your horse's back move up and down as she moves from one diagonal pair of legs to the other; do you feel both halves of her back moving forward and backward very slightly? Again, as with the walk, try to become aware of feeling how your horse moves in the jog but don't emphasize or exaggerate any movement. Just try to be aware of and feel her movements, as well as how they move your pelvis.

Lope

The lope is a three-beat gait followed by a moment of suspension when all four feet are in the air at the same time. If you're on the right lead, the pattern of footfall will be left hind, then right hind and left front together, then a push off from the right front, followed by a moment of suspension before the left hind touches the ground again.

Before a horse's leg can come under her body, the barrel must swing out of the way, as shown.

In the four-beat walk, the front and hind legs on the same side move in sequential order. Note, though, that the horse's head should not be carried below the withers.

Diagonal pairs of legs move together in the jog.

TIMING YOUR TRANSITIONS

The easier you make it for your horse to do what you're asking, the greater the likelihood you'll become partners who move together effortlessly. When you ride as partners, riding becomes more like ballroom dancing and less like just getting from here to there. Once you become aware of the position of your horse's feet, the sky's the limit as to how you use this tool to become one with your horse. Here are some ideas to get you started with transitioning from the walk to the jog and from the walk to the lope. We'll also discuss downward transitions.

Walk-Jog Transition

Because you won't be posting (rising out of the saddle in time with either front foot) at the jog, it's not as crucial to time your cue to a certain foot when you transition from the walk to the jog. However, it is helpful to ask for the jog from the walk as a foreleg is landing. First, cue for the jog

as the right front foot comes to the ground. This will occur while the barrel swings right (the same side as the front foot you're timing to your cue). Because the opposite (left) hind leg will be coming off the ground, it's a perfect time to ask for the push off to the jog with that diagonal hind leg.

Walk-Lope Transition

To pick up the right lead, for example, apply your cue to coincide with the left hind's coming to the ground. An easy way to pick up the right lead is to start cuing with your left leg at the apex of the barrel swing to the left and to follow it to the midline of the swing. Cuing here will help influence the left hind leg and create the first step of the right-lead lope.

Downward Transitions

On any downward transition, such as from lope to jog or from jog to walk, you can time your request to coincide with the outside hind foot as it is in the

The lope is a three-beat gait followed by a moment of suspension when all legs are in the air, as shown.

air. Doing this helps keep your horse from falling on her forehand in the transition and gives you a precise moment to time your cue. It will take practice to perfect your timing and set both you and your horse up to transition at a certain phase of her stride, but the awareness you gain will help you develop your skills of timing and feel.

Whatever gait you're in, get in time with the outside hind leg, which will vary depending on which direction you're going in a circle. If you're riding a straight line, pick either hind leg as the "outside leg." Start with the walk and become aware of where your horse's outside hind foot is in space. Remember that it will be coming off the ground as her barrel swings to the apex of the same side as her outside hind. Let's say you're asking for a halt from the walk, and her outside hind at this moment is her right hind. Notice when her barrel swings and when her right hind is coming off the ground, then add your cue to halt when this foot is in the air. Imagine your horse planting that outside hind foot and stopping on it as it lands on the ground. With practice, you'll be able to do it.

Use that feeling and imagery in the jog and the lope, and time your cue to stop when the outside hind is in the air. It may take a few strides to get the hang of this, but practice will bring you closer to having this foot initiate the downward transition.

HAVE FUN WITH FOOTFALL

Timing cues to certain footfalls is advanced work that will help you be a better rider for your horse. It may be challenging to correctly pick the timing every time, but you will become proficient with practice. To be most effective, be sure you're centered, don't hold your breath, and relax as you ask for a transition. Otherwise, you will put you and your horse out of balance.

But don't be afraid to make mistakes. If something doesn't work very well, try something else. If something does work, try to remember what you did and attempt it again. Your horse will let you know when you're on the right track by becoming softer, lighter, and more responsive.

In the walk-lope transition, the rider gives the cue when the out side hoof is coming to the ground.

Moving Beyond Cues and Aids: The Inner Aspects of Riding

You can and will make great strides in your riding ability by concentrating on improving your balance, seat, and hands and by refining your aids and cues. But there's more.

Breathing correctly and consistently can affect your horse in a powerful way. In addition, seemingly esoteric actions of focus, awareness, and intent can give you many positive results if you choose to use them. Riding from your center can lead to greater physical and mental connection with your horse. These more subtle aspects of advanced riding can take you to even higher skill levels. Their applications can last a lifetime, and they can also bring you benefits in other parts of your life. Here are some tips on integrating these ideas into your riding.

BREATHING

If we don't breathe, we don't live very long! While breathing is automatic, correct breathing may be something you need to work on. Your breath should have the same rhythmic flow as the quiet ticking of a metronome, no matter what's going on around you.

As mentioned previously, strive to breathe more into your belly and lower ribs rather than high in your chest. The benefits are more oxygen and a technique to help quell anxiety during stressful times. The benefits for your horse are that you become a calm, trustworthy presence that can help her during a quick spook, in a new and overstimulating environment, or when a storm kicks up on a trail ride.

Horses hold their breath when they're startled or worried, just as we do. Just for fun, the next time your horse seems nervous or is not

Here a horse is on high alert. Slowing and regulating your breathing when your horse is reactive can help her settle and calm down.

focused on you, pay attention to your breathing. Where is it? Is it high in your chest? Is it shallow and quick? Are you holding your breath? See if you can bring your breathing back down to your ribs, slow its tempo, and time it to your horse's strides. See if your change to low, rhythmic breathing helps your horse regain her own calm breathing and helps her settle.

Pilates, yoga, aikido, tai chi, meditation, and other methods that use focused breathing can help you learn to control and use your breathing to help your riding. Over time and with diligent practice, correct breathing will become automatic and positively affect your riding and your life.

FOCUS

What should I fix for dinner? Hey, could you walk through the puddle rather than jumping over it? Are we out of milk? Would you please not crowd the horse in front of us? He might kick! I've got to pay the car insurance bill. I wonder what mood my boss will be in tomorrow. Would you please quit diving for grass? You're yanking my arms out of their sockets! I've got to remember to pick up the dry cleaning on Wednesday. Whoa! I've had enough with your jigging and head tossing!

Does that internal monologue sound like one you've had while riding? Many riders, even those with quite a bit of experience, tend to get upset when they think their horses aren't focusing on them. But to be fair, their horses are focusing on them just as much as they are focusing on their horses. The problem is that neither partner is fully focused. It's rather uncanny how a horse's attention span exactly matches that of her rider.

Human beings tend to think in scattered ways and believe they are efficiently multitasking when doing so. However, think about the folly in multitasking. Is it really possible to do two things at once, fully and completely? No, one activity will have more thought directed to it than the other will. The second activity may get accomplished, but it might not be done as well as it could have been.

Horses live in the present, in the here and now. When we choose to be with them, we should strive to be with them mentally as well as physically. The next time you ride, play a game with yourself and count how many times you start thinking about your grocery list, the phone calls you need to return, your plans for dinner, and so on. You might be surprised.

When you're riding, let riding be the most important activity at that moment. Put aside the other cares of your day, and focus on working with your horse. Changing your thoughts so you are mentally present with your horse can be challenging, but the rewards are huge. The result will be a horse that's more focused on you because you're more focused on her. It's also likely you'll have less trouble with spooking or other unwanted behaviors because you are with your horse at every step. You will be able to defuse worry and distractions because you will feel them start before they escalate into full-blown spooks or other unwanted actions.

Start working on your focus in your hours spent out of the saddle by completing one task before moving on to another. Try noticing the details in the task. What are the efforts involved in doing that task? Spend a few minutes a day being present in each moment rather than thinking forward to tasks you need to do or rehashing events from the past. Start small and build on your successes.

AWARENESS

Have you ever driven from one place to another and arrived safely but had no recollection of the trip? Many people go through life in a daze, unaware of their surroundings. This state of distraction can get you into trouble if, for example, you don't see the brake lights come on in the car ahead of you in time to stop.

When you're with your horse, your awareness can also keep you out of harm's way. You'll notice situations or obstacles that may cause an accident, and you can take care of them before they cause harm. You'll be alert to changes in

your horse's behavior that tell you something is wrong, whether it's a minor bout of colic, the start of lameness, or the first signs that your horse is about to pull back in the crossties because something startled her.

Make a game of increasing your awareness. As you go for a walk, take mental notes of people's clothing, hair color, and height. As you're driving, remember car colors, license plate numbers, and numbers of passengers. Recall those details a few minutes later.

While riding, shift your awareness to how your horse is responding while also staying aware of your surroundings. If you're riding in an arena with others, keep an eye on what's going on so you can avoid trouble. Ride with the flow rather than against it. With time, you'll find that your awareness in all parts of your life is improving.

INTENT

Because horses evolved in an environment where noticing tiny differences meant survival instead of death, they are attuned to subtle changes and unspoken language. They can read the good intent behind a beginner's bumbling technique, and they can recognize malicious intent behind an abusive trainer's technique.

Here's the catch. If your intent is always to help your horse understand what you're asking and consider why she may not be responding, she will probably try very hard to do the right thing. If your intent is to force her to do what you say no matter what and with an element of threat, she will still probably try very hard to do the right thing.

To the untrained eye, the outcomes of both approaches may appear to be the same: The horse is doing what you ask. The differences lie in the long-term effects and the type of relationship that will result from the variations in the treatment of the horse. A relationship with a horse whose responses are based on a foundation of mutual respect and trust feels very different from one with a horse who responds from the fear of negative consequences.

A rider gets distracted by a call on his cell phone. He should be fully focused on his horse, if he expects his horse to focus completely on him.

Remember: You are the same person on and off the horse. Your intent and actions toward others—humans and horses—affect the quality and depth of your relationships with them. Whether you choose to create relationships based on cooperation or coercion is up to you. Just be aware that your intent has consequences.

CENTERING

You may have heard of the term "center" in relation to Pilates, core abdominal work, or correct lifting techniques. Your center is located about two inches below your belly button and in the middle of your body. As mentioned earlier, riding instructor/author Sally Swift brought us the concept of centered riding, which has given many riders the ability to move in sync with their horses and to learn to ride in a balanced and supported position.

Bring focus to your center as you ride and move from the energy in your center. Whether you want a transition or a change of direction, a change of tempo, or a change in the horse's

degree of collection, learning to ride from your center brings a new level of connection to your horse. Physically, this can help you sit with better balance. Because you'll initiate movement from your center, you'll be less inclined to lean forward or backward. Your movement will always start from your center. Riding from your center can also help you feel that you're sitting deeper in the saddle, with more stability and control.

Centering when you ride and during the other hours of your day assists you mentally by helping you remain calmer during stressful moments, think with more clarity, and stay focused on the task at hand rather than allowing your mind to race to all sorts of unrelated issues. Not surprisingly, centering also enhances your correct breathing, focus, awareness, and intent.

As with so many aspects of becoming an advanced rider, if you start to bring awareness to your center during your day, you will soon become more centered all the time—not just when you're riding. The benefits of this can extend to your job, your home, and your family.

CHAPTER 3

Advanced Schooling

*a*s you continue to increase your abilities as a western rider, you'll want to start training for more advanced movements than just the walk, the jog, and the lope. Remember that advanced schooling applies to you, as well as to your horse.

The movement you're looking for in your horse first starts with you, whether it's collection, backing, or a quick change of gaits. Your body and mind set initiate the change. In addition, bringing softness, balance, lack of bracing, and mental focus to your work will go a long way toward training in more advanced techniques. The advances that you and your horse can achieve are boundless if you keep a cooperative, positive outlook that says, "We can do this."

Following are some ideas to get you started with advanced techniques, including self-carriage, collection, softness, head position, smooth transitions, lateral work, and other areas.

Striving for Self-Carriage

Self-carriage may be a term you've heard used with English riding and dressage, but it applies just as much to the western horse and an advanced western rider. In true self-carriage, the horse carries himself in a balanced manner, through all gaits and transitions, without influence from the rider. The rider doesn't need to continually remind the horse to carry his head correctly or lift his back, for example.

A horse in self-carriage moves softly and quietly in a rounded frame and is able to respond quickly and effortlessly to requests from the rider because he is balanced, correctly aligned biomechanically, comfortable, and ready to do whatever his rider may ask. The western horse in self-carriage brings forth images of the *vaquero* spade-bit horses (see Chapter 4 for information on spade bits). After years of progressive training and correct riding, these finished bridle horses are extremely responsive to the bit, carry their necks and heads in positions that work best for them without any bracing or stiffness, are light in the front end, and are ready to change direction or speed in an instant. They work from tiny rein movements from the rider and present an overall picture of the western horse that's ready to do what's asked of him immediately and cheerfully.

No matter what discipline within the western riding genre you want to pursue, working toward

Here a spade-bit horse trained in the *vaquero* method displays the self-carriage desired in any western horse.

Horses (and riders) who use their bodies correctly will more easily put in a hard day's work, such as working cattle, than those that can't work in self-carriage.

self-carriage can help you attain the goals you're seeking to accomplish with your horse. For example, in a western pleasure class, the pair that is soft and round and whose work appears effortless will usually place well. The pair that's stiff and hollow and that relies on yanks on the reins to maintain a certain headset usually won't do so well. Although the modern western pleasure show horse is not the epitome of self-carriage compared with a correctly moving dressage horse or properly trained spade-bit horse, he should still carry himself in a good position rather than respond to the bumping of the bit or intimidation from the rider to maintain his position.

On a long trail ride or when bringing in cattle, the pair that moves together well, using their bodies efficiently and correctly, usually ends a long day in better physical shape than a pair with a rider who braced in the saddle all day or whose horse pushed against a tie-down all day.

Once again, good riding is all about the biomechanics of you and your horse. To work most effectively, efficiently, and comfortably, both of you should be soft yet supported in your bodies, move correctly for your conformation, and use only the amount of energy necessary without expending extra effort.

False self-carriage results from the rider pulling or bumping the horse's mouth to maintain a certain frame or headset, or using a harsh bit that the horse fears and avoids, or from the horse leaning on the reins or a tie-down as a form of support. False self-carriage is generally forced from the outside rather than flowing from the inside of the horse of his own accord.

This horse is behind the bit. False self-carriage comes from artificial means to achieve a certain headset or way of going.

To move well as a team, as shown here, horse and rider must develop the ability to carry themselves in a supported yet soft manner.

YOUR ROLE

Self-carriage in a horse actually starts with self-carriage in the rider. In fact, the horse can be seen as a mirror of the rider's self-carriage or lack thereof.

How do you attain self-carriage? Much of what we covered in Chapter 2 leads to human self-carriage. In a nutshell, it means you're not braced or locked in any of your joints and you allow your skeleton, rather than your muscles, to support you. When you do need to use muscle, you use only what you need and nothing more. Additionally, you feel the horse's rhythm.

For many riders, the first thing to think about in their own self-carriage is the position of their backs. Many people ride (or were taught to ride) with a slight arch in their backs. Some riders, commonly equitation riders, were taught that this makes them look as if they are sitting up straight, but, in reality their arched backs are hollow.

If we want our horses to travel with strong, lifted backs rather than hollow and arched backs, we must first ride with strong, lifted backs. If we

arch our backs, it's very likely our horses will arch theirs, too, to get away from the discomfort of the feel from our stiff, arched backs.

Our goal is to carry our bodies effortlessly in supported, soft, and correct manners and for our horses to learn to do the same. For us, this often stems from using our core correctly, which can take time to develop. Moving in self-carriage starts with being aware of how we affect the movements of our horses.

TESTING

When you're riding your horse and he's moving softly and well balanced, test to see if your horse is in self-carriage. To do this, keep your legs, seat, and upper body in the same position, but move your hands forward and release your rein contact with your horse's mouth. Ride for a few strides and notice what your horse does. Then pick up your reins again and continue on. You may want to try this a couple of times.

When you give the reins, what happens? If he carries on in the same softly balanced manner, then he is in self-carriage. If he rushes forward, falls on his forehand, pulls the reins out of your hands, or shakes or raises his head, then he's not.

When you take the reins back, does he poke his nose out or brace his back, neck, poll, or jaw? Does he toss his head? These actions also indicate he's not in self-carriage and is not comfortable with something about the way you're riding him. It could be the bit, dental issues, saddle fit, back soreness, your hands being hard (too heavy, rough, or insensitive), your body having

braces, or other areas that concern him when he's asked to use or carry himself more correctly and raise his back.

This test helps you determine your horse's balance and how his self-carriage is developing. If he's unable to stay in the soft, balanced frame that you started with, you know he's being held in position or influenced by you in some way. This is normal for many horses and riders who haven't yet developed the muscle and balance to attain self-carriage, so don't worry. Just keep working on it.

By keeping her body position but giving the reins for a few strides, this rider confirms that her horse is correctly in self-carriage.

Building on the Self-Carriage Foundation

A well-trained western horse that carries himself correctly is a picture of beauty and an example of the principle that form follows function. He's got a nice line from his withers to his poll that's either quite level or nicely curved, depending on his breed and conformation. He breaks naturally and comfortably at the poll; he covers ground well but doesn't rush; he travels straight; and he has a happy "let's get to work!" look on his face.

Although different show classes and breed requirements may call for slightly different looks, every western horse can benefit from the same foundation that helps a horse develop the ability to carry himself correctly. Let's take a look at the main areas.

COLLECTION

You may hear people say that "collection" means that a horse is going more slowly or taking shorter strides, but this is incorrect. A horse that is collected can be thought of as a spring that is being tightly wound. He raises his head from the base of his neck, telescopes his neck from his withers, and lifts his back so his legs can come more under his body. With true collection, this coiled spring develops an energy and eager explosiveness that is ready to be unleashed at the rider's suggestion. Because he's moving in a biomechanically correct way, the horse moves effortlessly. He's ready to go from a standstill to a gallop in a heartbeat, then slide to a stop, roll back, and gallop off in the other direction. He can change gait, direction, and speed in an instant because he's balanced and ready.

False collection is when a horse's back is shortened or hollow. No matter what his head and neck are doing, if his back is hollow and he's not lifting through his body, he's not truly

A calm, confident rider will develop the right mind-set to achieve their riding goals.

This horse softness actually comes from the inside and from an understanding and trust of his rider.

collected. In addition, traveling with false collection for many months or years can lead to pain issues in a horse's hocks, his back, and even his front legs.

SOFTNESS

Some horses are very responsive. In fact, they are so responsive they're almost like automatons. They offer up what they think you're asking of them very quickly, very mechanically. If you don't let them know that they've done something correctly, they may worry and offer another movement in quick succession, just in case the first movement wasn't the right answer. Horses responding out of fear or intimidation often look worried. Frequently, their faces and eyes show worry, showing up as wrinkles around their eyes or mouths. These horses may be responsive, but they're not soft.

But what does soft mean? Rather than responding reactively to your requests, a horse that's soft responds willingly, easily, and thoughtfully. He's not worried. Instead, he is thinking about what you're asking and offers his response

based on trust, not from fear of what might happen if he doesn't. Softness in a horse also allows him to respond very quickly and to seemingly imperceptible cues. He responds not with a frantic look but with one that is self-assured.

Softness, as with most aspects of advanced riding, starts with the rider. Actually, it comes from the heart of the rider—rather than the hands or the body—and with a commitment not to get into a fight or a pulling match or to train from a negative emotional state.

HEAD POSITION

A lot of show classes call for the horse's head to be in a certain position, often called a headset. In stock horse breeds, this usually means the neck is parallel to the ground, with the ears no lower than the withers. The head is flexed at the poll, with the nose either vertical or a couple of inches in front of the vertical. In other breeds, such as Arabians and Morgans, the conformation calls for more curve in the neck, with the head in relatively the same vertical position as the stock horse's head.

This is an example of a correct head position stemming from the horse's conformation and correct use of the hindquarters.

However, even if you never enter a show pen, a correct head position developed patiently over time (rather than forced from heavy hands or a harsh bit) enables a horse to carry himself in an efficient and biomechanically correct manner for his conformation.

Logically, you may think the head position comes from the front end; done correctly, however, it starts in the hindquarters. That's why it's not helpful—and actually can be harmful—to ask a horse to carry his head in a certain position before he's comfortable with lifting and lengthening his back, collecting, and moving with a soft, balanced full and forward stride. If you ask your horse to set his head by pulling on the reins, you'll jam him from front to back, and he'll often respond by going behind the vertical to avoid the discomfort of the bit. He will often hollow his back and shorten his stride, as well. All this can lead to pain and to training issues

related to pain. So when first working toward a nice head position, be less concerned about how your horse looks up front and more concerned with how he feels behind.

When a horse is moving correctly and with a lengthened topline, you'll feel him push from his hind legs. He'll be easy to steer and maneuver. If he's hollow in his back or has more weight on his forelegs, he'll feel heavy and hard to turn. If he's also raising his head, which usually goes along with a hollow back, he'll likely have short, choppy gaits, and his forelegs will hit the ground with more force.

The positions that a horse carries his head in the show ring can be misleading. His front end may look as if he's moving correctly, but if you look at the entire picture, you may see that his back is hollow. You can see whether the head position is right for the horse or whether he's in an artificial position imposed by the reins or the bit.

Smooth Transitions

As mentioned in Chapter 2, transitions get you from one speed to another within a gait, as well as from one gait to another. As with anything concerning riding, transitions can be done any old way just to get from point A to point B with little finesse. Or they can be used as an exercise in working together with your horse. Done well, transitions help a horse develop strength and athletic ability, and they encourage him to move in a balanced manner that leads to self-carriage.

For the rider, good transitions help develop body control and refined cues. The faster you go, the more difficult it can be to maintain good position. Practicing many transitions allows you to ride at a slower gait, then transition to a faster gait for as many strides as you can maintain correct position, then transition back to a slower gait before you lose position.

TRANSITIONS WITHIN GAITS

It's good practice—and it takes the monotony out of training—to vary your speed within the gaits. For example, try transitioning from a slow walk to a medium walk to a really ground-covering walk and back to a slow walk. Or pick up a jog, flow into a normal trot, then into an extended trot, and go back to a jog. Go from a lope, roll into a gallop, and move back to a lope again.

Doing transitions within each gait increases your horse's responsiveness to cues and helps you work on refining your cues so they become as small as possible. These gait variations also give you more opportunities to practice working with your horse as a team.

To speed up and slow down within each gait, start by getting in time with your horse's footfall and rhythm, which we covered in Chapter 2. Let's start with the walk. Remember to always start with the smallest cue possible and the cue you eventually want to end up using. You can always increase the pressure of the cue if you need to. Here, we'll just try to use a rhythm change to ask your horse to transition to a bigger walk.

Pick up a normal walk. Do you have the 1-2-3-4 rhythm in your head? Are you feeling the swing of the horse's barrel pushing your legs out, alternating right, left, right, left? Remember not to emphasize any particular movement in your body or exaggerate it; simply be aware of it.

Now, increase the tempo of the 1-2-3-4 rhythm a little. See whether you can get a bigger walk just by changing the rhythm of the tempo in your head. Keep breathing and stay soft in your body to allow for the extra movement your horse will need to make to increase his stride. This is advanced work, so it may not happen the first time you try it.

If he doesn't increase his stride with the change of tempo, gently use your legs to encourage him to pick up the pace. At the instant he starts to increase his stride, release the cue and let him continue on.

To slow down, bring the tempo in your head back to the beat of a more sedate walk and slow your body's movement. Think about how your body would transition to a slower speed if you were out for a walk; then use this same feeling to communicate with your horse. This is different from bracing and resisting to slow down. This is more like slightly slowing the movement of your hips and pelvis. Your horse may feel the difference and slow down to match your new pace.

Every horse is different. You will need to find what works best for you and your partner. There aren't any set rules here, so play and experiment to see how little you need to do to get the changes you're looking for.

UPWARD AND DOWNWARD TRANSITIONS

Basic transitions upward (halt to walk, walk to jog, jog to lope) and basic transitions downward (lope to jog, jog to walk, walk to halt) are good exercises to help your horse develop a more muscled topline and the ability to carry himself correctly. They also help increase the horse's responsiveness as he waits for your next cue rather than continuing on in a single gait for many minutes.

After you've perfected the basic upward and downward transitions, you can start working on transitions between gaits, such as halt to jog, halt to lope, walk to lope, lope to walk, and jog or lope to halt. Use the same ideas you have been exploring in transitions within the gaits, including increasing or decreasing the tempo of the footfall, slowing or speeding up the movement in your body, and changing your breathing to increase or decrease speed and tempo in your horse's gaits.

Lateral and Other Work

In addition to going in straight lines or around an arena, it's good to incorporate lateral and other advanced movements into your training. Lateral work means sideways movement, and it can vary from a slight sideways movement in a leg yield (while also maintaining forward movement) to an entirely sideways movement, such as in a side-pass.

Lateral work—as well as turns on the forehand and hindquarter, backing, and other advanced work—also encourages your horse to use his body correctly, as it's quite difficult to move in these ways if he's heavy on the forehand or braced in his body. In addition, lateral work helps you refine and clarify what you're looking for before you ask, so you know when to reward your horse. You'll become more in tune with each other as you refine these movements until you are able to ask for them with tiny cues.

With lateral work (and all work, for that matter), it's best to incorporate short periods of these exercises into your training rather than to drill them over and over. Drilling runs the risk of undoing your good training. If your horse is doing something well, you may want

Basic transitions (top photo) and lateral work (pictured) can help strengthen your horse.

to keep doing it because it's rewarding and fun. But asking him to continually perform the same task, may make him think he's doing something wrong. (Otherwise, you wouldn't keep asking him, right?) He may start changing what he's offering to see if another answer is the correct one, and you may just undo the good work that you have done by confusing him. Instead, ask for a few steps of a movement, get a good response, then reward him and move on to something else.

Remember that there are stages to teaching anything new, so you're not looking for perfection or for the entire movement to begin with. You simply want your horse to try to do what you're asking and to respond quietly. Slowly add more pieces of the movement while both of you stay soft and balanced.

Before you begin a movement, create a mental picture of what you're looking for. Imagine what this movement will feel like. Keep this picture and feeling in mind as you ask your horse for a movement; then reward the smallest effort in that direction. You may not get the entire movement the first time, so praise your horse for taking the first step or even thinking about or shifting weight in the correct direction.

BASIC PIVOT TURNS

When you ask for a turn on the forehand, your horse's front legs stay in the same general position while his hindquarters pivot around them. In a turn on the hindquarter, his forelegs pivot around his hind legs, which remain relatively stationary.

When you train for these movements, it's helpful to think of your reins as directing the front of the horse and your legs as directing the rear of the horse.

Turn on the Forehand

For a turn on the forehand to the left, your horse will move his hind legs around his front legs in a clockwise rotation. The pivot point is the right front foot, though he will need to lift and set down this foot from time to time so he doesn't

torque his leg. The left front foot will walk a small circle around the right front. The hind legs walk a circle around the front legs, with the right hind crossing in front of the left hind.

To ask for a turn on the forehand to the left, halt your horse and flex his head a little to the right by shortening your rein. Apply your right leg behind the cinch and ask him to move his hindquarters to the left. When he's learning, he may also need to move forward a little, but try to keep the forward movement as small as possible. As soon as he shifts his weight to the left or takes one step, release your cues and reward him.

Try again, building on that first step and rewarding him when he tries to offer movement that is close to what you're looking for. Eventually, he'll be able to take several steps with his hindquarters until he's able to complete an entire circle.

To ask for a turn on the forehand to the right, just reverse the steps and ask your horse to walk his hind legs to the right (counterclockwise), making a circle around his front legs.

Turn on the Hindquarter

For a turn on the hindquarter to the left, neck rein to the left; your horse will move his front legs around in a counterclockwise circle. His left hind leg will be his pivot foot, and his right hind leg will make a small circle around it. The front legs will move in a circle to the left, and the right front leg will cross in front of the left.

To make this motion easier for your horse, first ask him to shift his weight to his hindquarters. He doesn't need to take a step back, just shift his weight backward. As he does this, apply the neck rein and ask him to move his front legs to the left. Stay upright and balanced in the saddle and don't try to help him by shifting your weight one way or another or by adding leg to push his front end over. Again, reward him the moment he shifts weight to the left or takes one step. Build on his attempts by releasing all your cues. In time, your horse will be able to pivot an entire circle around his hind feet.

To ask for a turn on the hindquarter to the right, just reverse the directions. Your horse will move his front legs clockwise around his hind legs, and his right hind will be his pivot foot.

SIDE-PASS

You can combine the work you did in the turns on the forehand and the hindquarter to ask for the first steps of a side-pass. First, ask for a step of turn on the forehand, then a step of turn on the hindquarter, then forehand, then hindquarter, without pausing (but don't hurry) between the movements. Staying quiet and balanced is important. Then start to link these separate movements so they become a fluid single movement, transitioning to using light leg and rein aids at the same time to indicate to your horse the direction of the side-pass.

You can help clarify what you're looking for by positioning your horse over the end of a ground pole and asking for the side-pass so he needs to make only one step sideways before he is clear of the ground pole.

BACKING

Backing can be a useful exercise that helps build strength in your horse's back and hindquarters, and that helps him learn to raise his back and shift his weight from the front legs. It can also help your horse learn to carry himself forward in a round, soft manner, which will lead to self-carriage.

Help your horse learn to back softly, understanding what he is asked to do, rather than forcing the movement mechanically or without energy. But be aware: Done improperly, backing is a great way to start a pulling match and install a very big brace in your horse that will take a lot of work to uninstall! So start with the commitment to not pull or try to force your horse to back up.

Take mental inventory of your body throughout your backing movement. Many riders tense their backs, especially the shoulder blades, when asking their horses to move backward. This bracing transfers to the horse, which can lead to pulling, so stay soft. Some trainers use leg aids when asking horses to back, but we'll just use the reins. We want to preserve the leg aid as a cue for forward or sideways movement.

With your body relaxed, pick up contact with your reins, just enough so your horse drops his nose or otherwise softens to the bit. Repeat this a few times, rewarding him each time by releasing the contact. Pick up contact again, then fix your elbows to your sides so your hands are in one place. Avoid pulling on your horse to back him up. By creating a barrier to his forward movement with your quiet hands, you'll help him learn to back up himself instead of being pulled forward.

This is like self-carriage going forward, except that you're moving backward. He likely will drop his nose again and reward himself by releasing the pressure. Keep your hands stationary and maintain your mental image, as well as the feeling of moving backward. He may then poke his nose out and bump into the bit, thinking you will release him. Keep still and let him find his own release. Then, add a tiny bit more contact and wait.

Let your horse figure out the correct response to move backward; even a shift to the rear is something to build on. You're looking for your horse to step backward himself, and he may bump into the reins and back off a few times before he finds the answer you're looking for. Your reins are not pulling him backward but are creating a boundary of limiting forward movement if he initiates it.

If your horse has a big brace and lifts his head and tightens his neck in response to your request, help him by tipping his nose or bringing his nose to the side and waiting. The idea is to set him off balance a little so that he needs to move, then to direct that movement backward the instant it happens.

Staying soft and try not to brace yourself; you'll find that your horse will eventually learn to back himself up. He'll round up, shift his weight, and move his legs backward in diagonal pairs.

COUNTER CANTER

Counter canter is taking the lead contrary to the direction you're traveling. For example, when

The side-pass can be taught by first linking hindquarter and forehand turns. This is a full step of a side-pass.

loping a clockwise circle to the right, you would normally be on the right lead. With a counter canter, you will instead be on the left lead. The benefits of the counter canter for your horse include increased suppleness and responsiveness to your aids, and the benefit for the rider is the development of coordination. It also is a good exercise in preparation for flying lead changes.

Counter canter doesn't simply refer to being on the "wrong" lead, however. In a good counter canter, your horse is slightly bent in the direction of the leading leg. So, if you're circling to the right on the counter canter left lead, he will still need to bend slightly to the left. If he's bent to the right, he is on the wrong lead for the circle, which won't help him develop physically the way a proper counter canter will. This is advanced work, however, so don't expect your horse to be able to stay on the counter canter lead and bend slightly toward the leading leg when you first start asking for the counter canter.

There are several ways to ask for the counter canter, and you can increase the difficulty as your horse becomes more balanced and experienced. This movement also asks your horse to listen to your cues rather than picking up the lead dictated by the direction he's traveling in an arena. When you're first starting out, you'll need to help your horse understand that he's not wrong when he picks up the "wrong" lead you ask for. It's also best not to do small circles of counter canter early on. Initially, it is a difficult maneuver, and he may want to switch to the "correct" lead to maintain his balance on the circle.

Perhaps the easiest way to start a counter canter is to jog the short side of the arena, round the corner, and then ask for the counter canter for a few strides on the long side of the arena, praising your horse as he does so. Then, before you reach the next corner, return to the jog. Do this a few times so your horse understands he should take the lead you ask for.

Next, try maintaining the same counter-canter lead on a very shallow serpentine, down the long side of the arena. Before you head into the

Backing should be as soft and fluid as forward movement, as shown, not a result of pulling.

corner on the short side, pick up the correct lead. Then, keep this lead as you make another shallow serpentine down the long side. As you get to the next corner, stay in the lead and continue on.

When these maneuvers are easy to execute, you can add difficulty by picking up the correct lead while going into the corner before the short side of the arena. Keep this lead as you cross the short side and round the corner. Then go across the diagonal, still in this lead, and start a large circle at the other end of the arena. Keep your horse flexed slightly into the lead and complete the circle on the counter canter. This is more difficult to do because your horse will need to keep his balance on the circle. Start with large circles and gradually make them smaller. Eventually, try riding a true serpentine, staying in counter canter.

FLYING LEAD CHANGES

If you've ever watched your horse perform a sequence of lovely flying lead changes out in the pasture, you know these movements are completely natural for a horse. Flying changes of lead are required in reining, horsemanship, and western riding classes, and they are an essential part of some speed events, such as pole bending and barrel racing. The secret to getting your horse to perform a flying lead change is to correctly set him up for the change and then allow it to happen.

Many of us experience problems when asking for flying lead changes because we get in our horses' way somehow. Whether through imbalance, conflicting aids, timing, or pushing for the change rather than allowing it, we make the change more difficult than it needs to be. It's easy to make flying lead changes very technical and complex, requiring lots of leg aids, weight shifts, and abrupt changes of direction. However, all of this extra input generally just makes it more difficult for our horses. Instead of adding complexity, see if you can decrease complexity and make it easy for your horse to understand you. You can always go back and add cues if you need to.

Before you start working on flying lead changes, be sure your horse is comfortable with the counter canter on progressively smaller circles. This will help him gain balance and build the necessary muscles to support himself correctly. Be sure that he's comfortable picking up either lead equally, as a horse that finds it difficult to pick up one lead will find it difficult to change to that lead in midair.

When you're ready to try flying lead changes, envision a figure eight in the arena and pick the spot at the center of the figure where you want to change leads. Pick up a lope on a circle on one half of the figure eight and on the correct lead. Ride a lap or two so your horse is working softly and quietly. Be sure he's breathing rhythmically and in a relaxed manner. Horses sometimes hold their breath similar to how we do when we're under stress or anxious. Be sure you're breathing regularly, too, taking long, calm breaths. Try inhaling for three strides and exhaling for three strides, or whatever is comfortable for you.

Ride with your center pointing in the direction you're going. If you're traveling to the right, your center should be pointed around the circle to the right. As you round the circle, stay balanced in the saddle. When you start the middle of the figure eight, switch your center to the left, exhale strongly, and keep riding to the left on the other circle of the figure eight.

Your horse may just have done a flying change for you! If he has, keep riding and praise him profusely. If he hasn't done the change, he may switch leads as he continues on the circle, so that he is on the inside lead. Give him a few strides to see whether he switches. If he doesn't, bring him back to the jog, then pick up the lope

again. Try switching your center again, as you come to the center of the figure eight and before you start the other circle. If you don't get the switch, try again.

Be confident that he can do this and keep what you're looking for in mind. After a few tries, if he isn't getting the lead change, stop and do something else. Let him stop and catch his breath. Jog around the other end of the arena or go for a quick trail ride, then quit for the day. Just don't become frustrated or upset. He's not being bad or resisting what you're asking for; he's just confused or is having physical discomfort doing what you're asking. Try a flying lead change again tomorrow or the next day.

You can also break the command down further by asking for the lead change through a simple change of trot steps between the leads. Decrease the number of trot steps you take while asking for the lead change, then ask for the change in the same place. This may also help your horse understand what you're looking for.

Keep Things Interesting

Just as you would get bored walking on a treadmill at the health club day after day, your horse gets bored doing the same old routine day after day. Whether you're training for western pleasure, barrel racing, or cattle events, it will do you both good to experience an occasional change of pace from your everyday training schedules. Cross training and trail riding can be good ways to break a routine.

CROSS TRAINING

Cross training (working a horse in more than one discipline) helps a horse be a better athlete, develop a broader range of skills, and balance the physical demands on his body. In addition, you may just find that your horse is a natural in an area you haven't considered before. This is especially true if your horse just doesn't seem happy in his work, or if he is lackluster about his job, or if you feel resentment from him at being asked to do this form of work. He may be trying to tell you something.

That said, if your horse is content with his job, you should be mindful of which other disciplines you expose him to. For example, if you are aiming for high levels of western pleasure competition, you may not want to introduce your horse to pole bending or other speed events. Introducing him to cattle work, however, may be a great idea. Similarly, trying to practice western equitation on a speed-event horse may not be a good match, but endurance riding or competitive trail riding might give him a good diversion and a break from the clock and the all-out performance he's expected to give while in an arena.

Good basic dressage training will benefit any horse and help him become more supple and more responsive, plus it can help foster a stronger partnership between you and your horse.

Your western horse might like to take his turn as a hunter with English tack. Horses can tell the difference between types of tack and will know to jog in a western saddle and a curb bit or to trot in an English saddle and a snaffle bit. Rather than ruining his abilities in one area, cross training can give him a fresh outlook so he goes back to his primary job with more zest.

TRAIL RIDING

Heading out of the arena can do wonders to improve your and your horse's outlook and attitude. You can take a break from the rigors of regimented training and enjoy each other's company.

If your horse has rarely been out of the arena, take it slow or he may become completely overwhelmed—just the opposite effect of the relaxing trail ride you envisioned. If he's a newcomer to trail riding, start by working him in the arena, then take him outside for a few minutes afterward to cool down. He should be a bit tired,

more relaxed, and able to enjoy the short trip. Once these trips become commonplace, you can start increasing the length of time you're out and the distance you travel from the barn. Eventually, you can travel a long distance from your horse's home environment, and he'll be secure about leaving, confident that he will be coming back.

If your horse is comfortable going a distance from the barn, consider hauling him to a trail where you can explore new sights for a few hours. For the first few times, going with an experienced friend who has a calm trail horse can help your horse adjust to the wide-open spaces. Just be sure the other rider understands your need to go slowly and to expose your horse to new things gradually.

If you have access to an open field, practice some nice transitions and flying lead changes as the terrain dictates. Side-pass over a log, do a turn on the forehand, back up to move through two bushes, or ask for a bigger walk to get to the next gully. Having real obstacles to negotiate gives your requests real-world applicability and helps increase your focus. Working outside helps your horse to develop confidence, surefootedness, and athletic ability—traits that benefit any horse in any discipline.

Keep in mind that a trail ride isn't an excuse to abandon your expectations for your horse's behavior or your consistency in riding your horse. You can still ask your horse to avoid snatching grass along the trail, to work in a soft and balanced manner, and to respond promptly to your requests. You can still ride your horse with as much awareness as you have while training at home. By all means, enjoy the scenery, but keep your thoughts on your horse and how he's responding. In the event something startles him, you will be with him mentally and be able to help him calm down rather than be caught off guard.

Opposite page: Cross training can include anything that's a change of pace: trail riding, jumping or working cattle.

CHAPTER 4

Equipment

*a*t first glance, most western tack looks pretty similar. Most saddles have horns and substantial skirts; the bridles often have ear pieces or browbands (but rarely nosebands), and usually some form of shanked bits.

Look a little more closely, however, and you'll start to see differences. The design and functionality of the saddle you need for the show pen differs from the saddle you need for roping. As for bridles, the tradition of each discipline, individual breed preferences, and local styles often influence what you'll use. Your choice of bits will depend on your horse's age and level of training, and it will depend on the events you ride in, as well as your horse's preference.

In this chapter, we'll examine the importance of saddle fit and how it can affect your horse's performance and soundness, as well as the ways in which saddle geometry can help or hinder your efforts to sit correctly on your horse. Then we'll move on to discuss bridles and bits and the specifics of tack for different events.

Basic Saddle Fit Guidelines for Performance

No matter your goal for yourself and your horse—whether it's winning in the show ring or spending as many hours out on the trails as possible—your horse won't be able to give it her all if she's in pain because of a poor saddle fit. A saddle that doesn't fit can cause all sorts of problems that may, at first glance, appear to be training issues.

The horse may be hard to catch and to saddle; she may show reluctance at having the cinch tightened; she may buck, bolt, shy, rear, or refuse to go forward; and she may have difficulty

picking up the lope or a certain lead. Saddle fit problems can start with back pain, but your horse may begin compensating in other areas. In addition to back or rib pain, she may also develop problems in the shoulders, lumbar area, hocks, and forelegs.

You may hear some riders say that they ride only for an hour or less or weigh only 130 pounds, or they provide some other explanation for why they don't worry about whether their saddles fit. However, think about if you were wearing a hiking boot that had an exposed nail poking through your sock or a small rock rolling around the inside. If you're only going for a thirty-minute hike, does the duration of your walk mean the nail or rock will hurt you less?

The following guidelines evaluate saddle fit (both with the conventional tree or without it) and reasons the saddle must fit both you and your horse.

ELEMENTS OF BASIC SADDLE FIT

When you're shopping for a saddle, you may hear that the saddle fits if there is sufficient clearance over your horse's withers—say, three fingers. It's true that no part of the saddle should press down on your horse's sensitive withers. However, wither clearance is only one aspect of good saddle fit; you need to look at the saddle trees and the bars, as well.

The saddle tree (the wooden or plastic frame upon which the saddle is built) causes a saddle to fit well or poorly, depending on how it is designed. All the fancy leather tooling or silver conchos added to a saddle won't help it fit if the tree isn't the correct shape for your particular horse.

Three elements of a saddle tree make it fit: rock, flare, and twist. Rock allows the tree to follow the horse's back as it rises and falls. Flare allows the shoulders to move freely and lets the saddle clear the loins to prevent pressure. Twist is the angle at which the bars of the tree are attached as they run parallel to your horse's spine.

In addition, the bars that lie parallel to your horse's spine are attached to the swells in the

A cinchy horse registers discomfort by swinging his head toward the rider (above). Pain from a poorly fitting saddle can result in many unwanted behaviors.

This saddle doesn't adequately clear the horse's withers.

front and to the cantle in the rear. Because the bars make contact with your horse's back along its entire length, they need to match your horse's back shape. They also need to be short enough that they won't extend past the horse's last rib and put pressure on the loins.

THE IMPORTANCE OF THE REAR CINCH

Although you may see a lot of riders, especially at horse shows, in saddles without rear cinches, they are important parts of the western saddle. When used correctly, a rear cinch can help increase the horse's comfort while wearing a western saddle.

The rear cinch is designed to keep the saddle comfortably in one position on the horse's back, rather than rocking from side to side, bumping up and down, or driving into the shoulders or loins. A well-fitting saddle should sit quite securely, but a rear cinch will prevent the front rigging from inadvertently creating a single pivot point at the front of the saddle that can cause the back of the

saddle to lift up and down or pull the front of the saddle into the horse's shoulders.

Contrary to what you may have heard, the rear cinch should be fastened quite snugly rather than allowing it to hang down a couple of inches under the horse's belly. If it's hanging, it's not providing the support for the saddle that it was meant to provide.

Always fasten the front cinch snugly before tightening the rear cinch and be sure you have a connector attaching the front and rear cinch. If your horse somehow gets loose while you're saddling and you only have the rear cinch fastened, it can slip backward and act as a bucking strap. Using a connector prevents the rear cinch from slipping backward and causing discomfort or surprising your horse, which she might react to by bucking better than a rodeo bronc.

The rear cinch is vital if you do any roping work. When you dally (snugly wrap the rope around the horn), the rear cinch bears the

This saddle is equipped with a rear cinch, which helps keep the saddle in a comfortable position.

A rider checks for bridging under the saddle.

weight of the cow and will keep the saddle stable as your horse holds the cow.

If you don't want to use the rear cinch, use extra-long latigos (cinch straps) on both sides of the saddle instead of just on the near side, where you tighten the saddle. This provides the same stability as using a rear cinch and avoid creating a single pivot point. Run the latigo from the front rigging, down through the cinch, up through the rear rigging, back down through the cinch, and back up again to the front—to form a V shape before you tie it off as usual at the front rigging.

QUICK SADDLE FIT TEST

To test your saddle's fit, put it on your horse without a pad. If you're evaluating a saddle to purchase, first put a square of bed sheeting over your horse's back to keep the saddle clean. Run the palm of your hand under the front of the saddle, from the withers to the scapula (shoulder blade). There should be enough room to run your flat hand without feeling that your hand is being pinched between the saddle and your horse.

Then, put your flat hand, palm side down, underneath the saddle and feel for even contact along the bars. Are there any gaps with little or no contact? Often these gaps can occur in the middle of the saddle—right about where you sit. This is called "bridging," in which the bars of the saddle form a bridge on top of your horse's back, making contact in only four places: two at the front and two at the back. This can be extremely painful.

Finally, check for some clearance between the rear edges of the bars and your horse's back. Is there some space over your horse's loin on each side, or is there a lot of pressure? Do the edges of the bars seem to dig into her loins? Are the saddle skirts short enough that they don't rub your horse? Skirts that are too long, which are sometimes found in western pleasure and equitation saddles, can cause painful rubbing and restrict your horse's hindquarter movement.

There should be no pressure or contact from the saddle along your horse's spine, so ask a friend or your trainer to check that the gullet is clear from the withers to the loin when you are sitting in the saddle.

After you ride, there should be an even area of sweat on your horse's back. Dry spots can indicate areas of pressure, or areas of no

The skirts on this saddle allow adequate space for the horse's loins.

contact. Look for her back to be smooth when you lift off the saddle. Any rubbed areas, frayed hair, lumps, or bumps are signs of pressure and friction. Also, look at the bottom of your saddle. The fleece lining on the underneath area of your saddle will be compressed or worn in areas of pressure points.

Using additional pads can't help a poorly fitting saddle fit better. (Adding another pair of socks to your hiking boot with the nail in the inside sole doesn't get rid of the pain of the nail; it just adds more pressure to your entire foot.) However, because western saddles are designed to be used with a pad or a blanket, be sure the pad you use helps, rather than hinders, the fit of the

saddle. Using a pad designed with more clearance over the withers is a good idea because the clearance helps keep the pad or blanket from shifting and putting pressure on the withers. Pads or blankets with sticky panels can help keep saddles from moving excessively, although a well-fitting saddle should stay in good contact with the horse's back without a sticky pad.

If you find that your saddle bridges, try using a firm foam like neoprene as a temporary measure to shim the bars where they lack contact. This will help provide more even contact along the entire bar without adding pressure in other places. However, shimming is no substitute for a well-fitted saddle.

FIT WITH TREELESS SADDLES

To avoid potential problems that can be caused by ill-fitting saddle trees, some manufacturers have designed treeless saddles. However, treeless saddles are not the perfect solution for every horse's saddle-fit issues. Some treeless designs work very well for some horses, while other horses don't find them comfortable because of their conformation. Keep in mind that even saddles without trees can produce pressure. We live with gravity every second of every day, so your weight in the saddle is always pressing down someplace. Whether it's pressing down on a traditional tree, on a foam pad that spreads across the horse's entire back, or on four pivot points, the saddle must make contact with the horse's back somewhere.

The secret to good saddle fit is finding a saddle—treed, treeless, or a combination of designs—that fits your horse's particular back shape. It should allow her to work comfortably and happily without pinching, bridging, rocking, or putting pressure on her withers, spine, scapula, or loins.

RIDER FIT CONSIDERATIONS

When looking for a new saddle, consider how it will help or hinder your efforts to be a better rider. Although there are many styles of saddles, good riding is good riding and good position is good position. Whether you're riding a reining horse, a roping horse, a gymkhana horse, a western pleasure horse, or a trail horse, the same basic position will serve you well (although there will be variations in position for different sorts of work). For example, a gymkhana or speed-event rider will have a more forward position than a western pleasure rider. However, the basic position is balanced with your head, shoulder, elbow, hip, and ankle aligned.

Look for a saddle with the lowest point of the seat located in the middle of the seat. In many saddles, the low point is set too far back. Even if you're the most balanced rider, when the lowest part of the seat is toward the rear of the saddle, your legs

This is an example of a chair seat, in which the lowest part of the seat is toward the rear of the saddle rather than in the middle. This causes the rider's legs to be pushed forward rather than balanced correctly under the hips.

will want to go into a chair-seat position, out in front of you rather than balanced correctly under your hips. You will struggle to ride in balance.

In addition, look for stirrups that are attached so that they hang straight down when you're in the saddle. In some saddles, the stirrups are attached too far forward, and you'll be continually struggling to avoid riding in a chair seat with a saddle like this.

You may see some riders braced up against the cantle with their legs shoved forward, and you may see this way of riding in some disciplines more than others. A rider may sit this way because the saddle is too small and there's no room for him or her to sit correctly in the middle of the saddle. Or it may be because the seat rises sharply or the swells make the rider bump into the front of the saddle when the rider sits in the middle of the seat. Another reason may be that the saddle is forcing the rider into a chair seat,

This rider is braced against the cantle with his legs jammed and braced in the stirrups, and he has a lot of brace in his right arm. This is not comfortable for either the rider or the horse.

so the rider overcompensates by bracing on the stirrups and jamming them forward to gain a (false) sense of security. The rider may have back or pelvic pain, and this position may have started as a subconscious attempt to relieve the pain.

No matter what the cause, this braced position is not comfortable for the rider or the horse. Remember the discussion on balance and seat in Chapter 2? The braces used by a rider in this position use a lot of extra muscle power, leading to fatigue and possible pain. Some riders may ride this way—as if bracing for the worst possible outcome—in an effort to stay on the horse. They may do this subconsciously or out of habit or fear. It may stem from the rider's biomechanical needs or the saddle's geometry. However, consider how such stiffness hinders a rider's ability to stay aboard. It actually causes a rider to lose balance, resulting in a much greater likelihood of falling off. Riders then subconsciously compensate for this by using even more grip and extra muscle power to stay on.

For instance, imagine a mannequin sitting on top of a horse. This "rider" will be stiff, without movement in the joints. Even if our plastic rider were able to grip as hard as possible with her knees or thighs, the stiffness and lack of mobility will likely cause the rider to fall off if the horse starts bucking or spooks, because she will be fighting against the movement rather than going with it.

Now imagine a rider with flexible joints, sitting balanced and using her skeleton—rather than muscle power—to stay on her horse. If her horse starts bucking, her body will be able to go with the horse's movement, and she likely will be able to stay on. Think of rodeo bronc riders. Do they sit braced and motionless as they ride their twisting, twirling, jumping partners in this eight-second dance? No, they move with the broncs' gymnastics.

In other words, strive to become the best rider you can be: balanced, fluid, and flexible but supported. Don't expect your saddle to lock you into a position or make up for your lack of balance. Only good riding, body awareness, and hours in the saddle can help you become the best rider you can be. However, do yourself a favor and find a saddle that helps you be the best rider you can be without being forced to overcome the incorrect positioning caused by a saddle that doesn't fit you.

Event-Specific Saddles

As we mentioned earlier, good basic riding position doesn't change drastically, no matter what your riding discipline. Although there are some differences in saddle design that allow for the needs of different events, your overall balance and position remain the same.

In addition, saddle manufacturers may have different criteria for what constitutes, say, a cutting saddle or an equitation saddle. Therefore, it's a good idea to try several saddles from different makers to be sure you find one that you and your horse like.

CATTLE WORK
The saddle required for working cattle is geared more for safety and functionality than for appearance. Roping a calf during a team roping competition or pulling a steer out of a muddy gully requires extra-stout saddle trees and horns, secure rigging, and a rear cinch. Roping saddles often have fairly tall and thick horns to dally the calf or the steer. A low, rounded fork reduces leverage against the horn and the horse's withers, and it allows for freedom of movement for the rider.

CUTTING
A cutting horse follows every move of a wily bovine trying to return to its herd. Therefore, a cutting saddle must allow the rider to stay in balance but without interfering with the horse's quick movements. With a generally flat seat; high swells; and a tall, thin horn, a cutting

saddle helps the rider stay in contact with the horse while maintaining a relaxed position, and it keeps the rider from slipping forward. The saddle often has narrower stirrups than an equitation saddle, so the rider sometimes has the stirrup against the heel of the boot.

REINING

Because reining is an event that rewards precision, it requires a saddle that is designed to optimize the horse's balance, natural athleticism, and freedom of movement. The saddle must also allow the rider to sit on the horse in proper balance while the horse is galloping circles, spinning, and sliding. Reining saddles are designed to allow the rider to feel the horse as much as possible. The horn is lower so it won't interfere with either the rider's hands or the reins. The seat is shaped to allow the rider to roll his or her pelvis back for making sliding stops.

SHOW RING

Many show saddles have suede seats, which—combined with your show chaps—really add grip and help you stay nearly motionless in the saddle. Judges like to see this lack of movement in equitation classes, and a quiet picture is also an advantage in pleasure and horsemanship classes. Today's show ring saddle often has a moderately built-up seat in the front with a low cantle and a short, fat horn. Show saddles often have intricate carvings and lots of silver.

SPEED EVENTS

A speed event saddle helps a horse move effectively and quickly, and it helps the rider stay out of her way. These saddles often have deeper seats than cutting or reining saddles and round skirts so they don't interfere with a horse's use of her hindquarters. They are often very lightweight and have a low horn.

Lightweight speed event saddles may have rounded skirts or shorter skirts than on show saddles.

For trail riding, use any saddle that's comfortable for you and your horse.

TRAIL AND PLEASURE

Trail and pleasure saddles are designed for trail riding—with comfort and support in mind. Usually more plain than show saddles, saddles for trail riding or pleasure riding can have any combination of horn, swell, seat, and skirt styles to fit to the needs of the rider. Generally light in weight, trail and pleasure saddles often have a slightly undercut fork, which is comfortable for long rides. The cantle is frequently higher than it is on other saddles, and it has a more pronounced dish. Some trail saddles have horns; others, such as endurance saddles, do not.

Western Bridles and Bits

Depending on which type of western riding you do, you may choose between several different types of headstalls, reins, and bits, as well as different types of bitless bridles, such as bosals and hackamores. If you show, just be sure your bridle meets the requirements in the rule book for your breed or association. Here's a look at what's available and appropriate for different styles of western riding.

HEADSTALLS

The headstall is what holds the bit or the bosal. The bridle is the entire set of tack that goes on the horse's head, including the headstall, the bit, the bosal or the noseband, and the reins.

For functionality, almost any type of headstall is acceptable as long as your horse finds it comfortable. In your area, you may see horses and riders using browband headstalls, one-eared headstalls, or split-ear headstalls, with or without throatlatches and usually without nosebands.

Headstalls may be made of leather, BioThane® (a synthetic material popular with endurance and trail riders), nylon webbing, waxed cotton, or braided rawhide. Headstalls may be fancy with lots of silver work or leather tooling or

The type of reins you use depend on the type of riding you do and the traditions associated with it. These are roping reins.

both, or they may be very plain with no extra ornamentation.

Headstalls used with a bosal or a hackamore-type noseband are often just a simple leather hanger that holds the bosal in place.

REINS

The type of reins you choose will be influenced by the type of riding you do and by local or breed traditions. The three main varieties of reins are romal, split, and reining.

Romal Reins

These closed reins are joined together near the point at which you hold them with your rein hand, keeping your fingers in a fist and closed around the reins. Where the two reins come together, there is a single length of leather about three feet long with a leather popper on the end. This is held on the thigh with the other hand, and many show rule books specify that there must be sixteen inches between your rein hand and the hand holding the single rein with the popper.

Split Reins
Just as the name implies, these reins are separate, not joined in any way. The rider can use them for direct reining, with a rein held in each hand; lap the reins together over the horse's neck and hold them in two hands; or hold them in one hand with the palm down and one finger between the reins.

Roping or Gaming Reins
These consist of a single rein and are shorter than romal or split reins. Riders who rope or run speed events don't want to worry about dropping them or having reins so long that their horses could step on them.

HACKAMORES, BOSALS, AND BITLESS BRIDLES
Originating from the Spanish *vaquero* (cowboy) tradition of training, a hackamore is a shaped noseband used alone with a hanger and attached to a pair of mecate reins. A mecate rein, often made of horsehair, uses a single length of rein about twenty-two feet long that combines reins and a lead rope. The hackamore rider uses two hands on the reins, and the nosepiece applies light pressure to the opposite side of the horse's face.

In comparison, a bosal is a thinner hackamore used under the bridle during the two-rein stage of training a horse to the spade bit (see the section on spade bits later in this chapter). In her training to be a spade-bit horse, a horse may wear a snaffle and a bosal and two sets of reins as she transitions from the snaffle to the bosal, then wears a bosal and a curb bit, and finally wears a bosal and a spade bit. Hackamores and bosals are usually made of braided rawhide, and well-made ones are soft and easily shaped to a horse's head.

This is an example of split reins in use.

A true hackamore or bosal is very different from a mechanical hackamore, which is one type of bitless bridle. A mechanical hackamore can be a cruel contraption, with long shanks, a narrow metal noseband, and metal under the horse's jaw. Some mechanical hackamores can break a horse's nose cartilage or her jaw. However, badly fitting or improperly used bosals can also cause damage. If you want to ride in a mechanical hackamore, choose one with has a fleece-lined, flat leather noseband, short shanks less than four inches long, and a curb strap instead of a curb chain.

Other bitless bridle styles can be good training tools. These include the jumping hackamore and the sidepull. The jumping hackamore usually consists of a leather noseband (or leather-covered rope) and has two rings for the reins near the level of your horse's mouth. It has a soft curb strap and is used like a hackamore but functions more like a snaffle with direct rein action.

A sidepull is often made with a lariat noseband (or two lariat nosebands), which is left plain or covered in leather. The lariat ends are often knotted at side rings where the reins attach. The knots are believed to give the horse additional signaling, much as the knots on a rope halter do.

BITS

Western horses may wear many different bits depending on the riding discipline, your horse's age and her level of training. Bits can include snaffles, curbs, or combination bits. Or you may commit to the years of correct and tactful training necessary to enable your horse to wear the spade bit, which is a bit based on finesse, not force.

Snaffle Bits

Many riders believe that a snaffle bit is some sort of jointed mouthpiece. Actually, a snaffle bit is any bit that doesn't use leverage but rather uses pressure on the horse's lips and tongue as the signal. A snaffle can have a solid mouthpiece, such as a mullen mouth, or a ported mouthpiece as well as a jointed mouthpiece.

If you are showing your horse, your breed or association rules may dictate that only horses under a certain age may be shown in snaffles (or in a hackamore), with the rider using two hands. Otherwise, the horse must wear a curb bit in competition.

Curb Bits

Simply put, a curb bit uses leverage. For many horse people, a curb bit means a ported bar mouthpiece with shanks of varying lengths; however, a curb bit can be any configuration of mouthpieces. The leverage action from the shanks is what makes it a curb bit, so even a jointed mouthpiece with shanks is still a curb bit.

When you apply pressure to reins attached to shanks, the bit rotates in your horse's mouth. It then makes contact with the curb strap or chain under her chin and can exert some pressure on the horse's poll. If the bit also has a jointed mouthpiece, it can make contact with the roof of your horse's mouth as well and put pressure on the tongue.

Combination Bits

Combination bits, which use jointed mouthpieces and shanks, are often considered transitional bits to take the horse from a snaffle to a curb. However, these bits (often called "Tom Thumbs" or "cowboy snaffles") are actually very confusing and can potentially inflict pain. Not only does the mouthpiece fold in the middle (which can poke the roof of a horse's mouth and pinch her tongue), but the shanks exert a huge amount of force on the jointed mouthpiece when the reins are pulled at the same time. This can result in real nutcracker-type action, placing tremendous pressure on the sides of the horse's jaw. In addition, the signals your horse receives are muddled.

With a true snaffle, you have direct rein pressure on your horse's lips and tongue. When you use a direct rein with a snaffle, you are pulling the horse's head in the direction you want to go; there also can be pressure on the opposite side of her face. With a true curb using a solid mouthpiece, there is leverage from the shanks to the chin and sometimes the poll, but the mouthpiece stays fairly level and quiet in the horse's mouth. Jointed mouthpiece curb bits combine all these actions and pull from the bit through the cheek-pieces and to the poll, adding up to many conflicting signals at the very least.

Spade Bits

With its high spoon port, braces, roller or cricket, and shanks, some people think that the spade bit is cruel. It isn't if it is used following years of soft and quiet work that bring you and your horse along in your education. When both of you have invested the years necessary to slowly graduate to working in the spade, it should be the ultimate tool of delicate communication, not an implement of force. Your horse has to be absolutely comfortable in the spade, though, or she won't be a successful spade-bit horse.

The spade bit gives the horse a lot of information. The rein chains connecting the romal reins to the bit signal to the horse that there's a request or change coming before any contact is made with the bit. This allows you to use tiny hand movements to ask for turns or differences in speed or gait. Although you may put some pressure on the bit at times, never pull your horse around with the spade or yank on her mouth.

Transition from Snaffle to Curb

This is a jointed snaffle.

Your horse may work well in a snaffle, a hackamore or another bitless bridle, and you may never need to transition to a curb bit. However, you'll want her to learn to go in a curb if you eventually plan to show, or if the riding you want to do, such as roping or reining, requires you to use one hand on the reins.

To help your horse transition from the snaffle to the curb, start with what she's familiar with and use the same equipment you've been using. If your horse can perform all the basics while in a snaffle or hackamore, such as stopping, backing, and turning, then start riding with your reins in one hand. It's traditional to ride with the reins in your left hand, whether you are right- or left-handed.

To teach your horse to neck rein, it helps to give her a reason to turn. Set up cones in the arena and walk patterns around them. Better yet, ride out of the arena into big open areas; turn around bushes, rocks, and trees; and negotiate gullies and other natural obstacles. Start by using the direct rein, but add the opposite rein across her neck. Turn only with the weight of the rein on her neck.

If she doesn't understand, you may need to use a direct rein at the same time, but never pull so that you're exerting pressure from the neck rein to the bit. Eventually, reduce the use of the direct rein and use only the indirect rein, as she starts to understand that the weight of the rein on her neck is your request for her to turn. Once she is responding and turning well with one hand on the reins, start her in a mild, short-shanked curb bit.

There are two schools of thought on moving a horse to a curb. One is that you have the basics down for neck reining, turning, and stopping in the snaffle or hackamore, plus you're riding with one hand. You then keep riding consistently this way, but you put your horse in a mild curb. Because you are using the same cues as you did with the snaffle

A

Curb bits such as these (A, B, C) use leverage from shanks of varying lengths, and the mouthpiece can be solid or jointed.

B

C

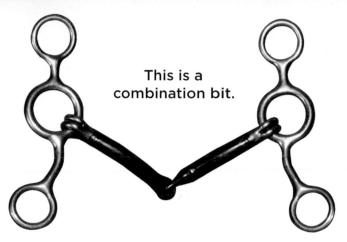

This is a combination bit.

When used correctly, as shown, the spade bit provides delicate communication to the horse, not pain or intimidation.

or hackamore, she will likely respond the same way and not be confused.

Another approach is to put her in a short-shanked pelham, with the same sort of mouthpiece eventually used in the curb. A pelham bit has rings for two sets of reins, and you ride with two sets of reins: the snaffle rein attached to the high ring of the pelham and the curb rein attached to the low ring of the bit. To transition, first ride her from the snaffle rein, which will give her the same direct lip and tongue pressure she learned in the snaffle. Over time, you'll start riding more from the curb rein, which will allow her to become accustomed to the leverage and action of a shanked curb bit. At this point, you can transition her to the curb bit of your choice and stop using the pelham.

Remember that the mouthpiece your horse likes best may be different from what you think she likes best, so be open minded. Some horses may like mild, thick mouthpieces with low ports, but horses with smaller mouths may find them too thick. They may prefer slightly thinner mouthpieces or mullen mouths. Changing to any new bit may, at first, cause your horse to chew on and play with the new bit. Let her wear the new bit without reins for ten minutes at the end of several rides, to adjust to it slowly. This will also tell you if she really is uncomfortable with the bit or is simply getting used to the newness.

No matter which way you choose, remember to envision what you're looking for before you ask and to stay consistent in your cues. The transition may take a few weeks or longer, but helping your horse stay calm and happy in the bridle will enable you to switch to the curb without fear or training issues because she hasn't been frightened by an unfamiliar bit that she doesn't understand.

CHAPTER 5

Ready to Compete

*a*s your riding skills advance, you may become interested in competing. Entering a competition can be a good way to monitor your progress.

You can choose from a variety of horse show classes, gaming and speed events, and cow events. Or you can explore other ways to have fun with your horse, including American Quarter Horse Association (AQHA) Versatility Ranch Horse competitions, competitive trail riding and endurance riding, cowboy mounted shooting competitions, games on horseback, and ride and tie events.

Just keep in mind that judged events are likely to be more subjective than timed events, in which the only deciding factor is the time on the clock.

When you show in front of a judge, one judge's opinion (or the opinion of a panel of judges) will determine on that particular day whether you win, place, or walk out of the ring without a ribbon. If you win, you'll likely be happy. But what if you have a great, flawless ride, only to be asked to exit with the rest of the riders who didn't place? Although you may be disappointed, remember that it's only that judge's opinion, and that opinion

may be different tomorrow, even if your ride is identical. To combat any feelings of frustration, it helps to view competition as simply a test against your previous best effort and a chance to receive subjective feedback on how you and your horse are doing as a team.

Always strive to do your best. If you know that you and your horse performed well as a team, then you should be proud. You will be a winner no matter what the judge says that day and no matter what placing you get in the class—even if you don't place at all. Ironically, putting more emphasis on the personal goal of doing well as a team with your horse, rather than setting out to win a ribbon, can lead to success in any competition. It's as if, once you let go of the importance of the outcome, you are freer to relax, ride well, and have a good time with your horse.

Winning is fun, no doubt about it. It's especially fun when you've done it by taking your horse

Equitation (shown here) and horsemanship classes judge the rider's ability.

into consideration and working as a team. At the end of the day, remember that you have a horse because you love him, you love riding, and there are few other ways you'd like to spend your time. When you keep these criteria in mind, you're always a winner.

One last point: Don't compromise your horse's well-being or happiness for a show-ring fad or to win a ribbon. In the best case, you will have sacrificed your ethics; in the worst case, your horse may suffer lifelong injuries or psychological damage.

No matter which area of competition you decide upon, conditioning your horse correctly for the event will help make the experience pleasant and increase your chances of doing well.

General Conditioning Tips

As with anything in life, the more prepared you are, the better the experience will be. Being well prepared physically and mentally will go a long way toward helping you and your horse enjoy the experience of competing and will enable you to place as high as you can.

When you're considering entering any competition, first consider what it will take to prepare for the event, then plan to spend the necessary time. If you're interested in competitive trail riding or endurance riding, check out conditioning books and other resources to set up a training schedule. It can take several months of consistent and increasingly strenuous training to be able to enter and complete a thirty-mile ride safely. If you want to try showing, allow enough time at home to train in the same things you'll be expected to do at the show. The show pen is not the place to work on the perfect lope or the sliding stop. Practice cattle work before you arrive at the event, so both of you are familiar with the rules and so you know how your horse responds to different situations.

Although practice and preparation are essential, don't drill your horse so much that he becomes soured and unhappy with the work you're doing. Running endless barrel patterns on your barrel horse, riding lap after slow lap in

A rider introduces his horse to cattle slowly and thoughtfully.

the arena on your western pleasure horse, and practicing the same handful of patterns on your reining horse can make him want to run the other way when he sees you coming. He knows it's just another day of the same old training. If he finds training stressful, he may start responding with pinned ears and a swishing tail, and it could escalate into rearing, running backward, bucking, and anything else he can do to get your attention and let you know he's not a happy horse. Instead, change things up. Add spice to your riding and choose not to follow the same riding and training routines day after day after day; your horse will thank you.

Finally, attend a few events without entering. Just travel to the grounds and unload. Let your horse eat from his hay bag. Walk him around or ride quietly. See if you can time a ride in the arena during the scheduled breaks in the schedule. This is a no-stress way to expose both of you to the sights, sounds, energy levels, and feel of a competition without the anxiety of entering. After a few calm hours, you can head home knowing you have prepared even more for your first entry into the world of competition.

Show Classes

Horse show classes run the gamut from reining and trail class to western equitation and western pleasure. Whether you're looking for something wild or mild, there's a show class for you and your horse to enjoy.

REINING

The reining horse and rider perform one of several predetermined patterns. Movements in each reining pattern include slow and fast lope circles; figure eights with flying changes; sliding stops; roll backs; spins; and a smooth, quick rein-back.

Reining competitions are based on the National Reining Horse Association (NRHA) guideline that states: "To rein a horse is not only to guide him, but also to control his every movement. The best-reined horse should be willingly guided or controlled with little or no apparent resistance and dictated to completely. Any movement on his own must be considered a lack of control." Therefore, your reining horse must perform the requirements of the pattern at your direction, waiting for your input rather than anticipating the next movement of the pattern. (Reining is shown in Chapter 3.)

Because attire is more casual than in many other show events, the reining rider typically wears a brightly colored shirt with a collar, a hat, jeans under chaps, and boots. Saddles and bridles are generally less flashy than those used in western pleasure and equitation. Horses can wear protective boots.

TRAIL CLASS

Originally designed to mimic the chores typically done by a ranch horse and rider, today's trail classes challenge entrants with creative obstacles combined with requested gaits between obstacles. A trail course may include a bridge or water crossing, low jumps, a gate, a mailbox, or a bag of cans to carry from one point to another. In addition, your horse may be asked to back through or side-pass around poles, perform a serpentine with lead changes, enter a box and turn around within it, jog or lope over a series of poles, and so on. You're judged on your horse's attitude, inquisitiveness, quietness, and confident ability to negotiate a variety of obstacles efficiently and without excessive hesitation.

You *can* show in working tack without a lot of silver; however, many show trail-class riders wear fancier outfits and tack than they wear in their other western divisions. If you use closed reins and are asked to ground tie, you may use hobbles.

WESTERN EQUITATION OR HORSEMANSHIP

In an equitation or horsemanship class, it is the rider who is primarily judged (rather than the horse) on her ability to produce a clean, quiet, and pleasing ride on her horse. The horse's performance is counted only as it reflects upon the rider's aids, balance, and position.

You are usually asked to walk, jog, and lope in both directions of the arena. You're also likely to be asked to ride a short individual pattern that will showcase your abilities. Patterns may be ultra-simple, such as jog to a cone, pick up a certain lead, lope for six strides and halt, then move back four steps. Or the pattern may be more complex; for example, jogging, then loping, doing a figure eight and performing a flying lead change. Some horsemanship classes may ask you to ride only an individual pattern, with no group work on the rail.

Generally, equitation and horsemanship riders dress more conservatively than those in western pleasure classes, but they still strive to make a positive impression on the judge. The look of a winning horsemanship pair is one that is planned to complement the horse's color, minimize the appearance of movement (equitation riders should appear glued to the saddle), and diminish rider body-type issues, such as large hips or short legs, while still making the pair stand out in a large class. Horses in equitation and horsemanship classes generally wear saddles and bridles adorned with lots of silver.

WESTERN PLEASURE

In the western pleasure class, the horse is primarily judged on being a pleasure to ride. (In contrast, in a horsemanship or equitation class, the rider is primarily judged.) Judges generally reward a horse for quality of movement, attitude, and manners.

In a western pleasure show class, you are judged at the walk, the jog, and the lope and are asked to go in both directions around the arena. Your horse is expected to keep a consistent tempo and use slow, easy gaits. His head and neck position differs depending on his breed, but he is expected to be quiet in the bridle, maintain a certain frame and speed without rein pressure, and respond quickly but quietly to requests for changes of gait.

The most basic attire requirements for riders in western pleasure classes are long pants, long-sleeved shirts, boots, and hats or protective headgear. Beyond this, there are regional differences, and the level at which you're showing will also influence what you wear.

A team negotiates an obstacle in a trail class.

A western pleasure rider typically wears chaps and coordinates the hat, tie, gloves, shirt, and saddle blanket to create a pleasing, unified picture for the judge. At higher levels of showing, such as breed shows at the regional and national levels, the attire can be really spectacular. Rhinestones, crystals, satin, spangles, bold colors, and patterns all vie for the judge's attention, as the rider hopes to stand out from the crowd.

Many competitors ride in saddles covered in silver: silver on the swells, silver on the skirts, silver horn caps, silver cantle plates, and so on. The idea is that, if you're as good as the other competitors, then the extra pizzazz will set you apart from the crowd and help the judge remember you and select you as the winner.

Horses can be shown in closed (romal) reins with no fingers between the reins or in split reins with one finger between the reins.

Gaming, Gymkhana, and Speed Events

For some riders, the beauty of competing in speed events is that it's all about the time on the clock. There are no judges' opinions, just the timer and you and your horse taking your best shot at the fastest time. Barrel racing, a combination of low jumps and pole bending called "bounce pony," "flag race," "keyhole," or "pole bending" are ways you can race with your horse to the finish line.

BARREL RACING

In barrel racing, you and your horse take a running start and negotiate a clover-leaf pattern around three barrels set in a triangle. (The Texas pattern has the barrels set in a straight line.) You can take the right barrel or the left barrel first. You finish by rounding the barrel at the far end of the triangle and racing back across the finish line. To make the best time, you need to be on the correct lead, make a straight line to the next barrel, and turn tightly and cleanly around all the barrels. If you knock over a barrel, you receive a five-second penalty. If you go off course, you are disqualified.

Barrel racing competitors usually wear jeans, boots, long-sleeved shirts, and hats. Women dominate this sport (even at the Pro Rodeo circuit level), and they wear flashier attire in the higher levels of competition.

Your horse's tack for barrel racing can be basic: a snaffle, curb, or hackamore bridle. Many barrel racers use saddles with round skirts to enable their horses to use their loins without being rubbed or pinched by longer square skirts.

BOUNCE PONY

Bounce pony is a race with cavalletti and poles. You and your horse jump a cavalletti and then bend around a pole. This leads you to another cavalletti. You continue on until you complete the course. The horse with the fastest time and the fewest faults wins. Missing the pattern, missing a pole, rapping a jump, or refusing a jump are all considered faults.

Most competitors wear jeans, boots, long-sleeved shirts, and hats. Your horse's tack can be basic, with a snaffle, a curb, or a hackamore bridle. You can use a saddle with a round skirt to enable your horse to use his loins without being rubbed or pinched by a longer square skirts.

FLAG RACE

In a flag race, a triangular pattern similar to that of the barrel race is used, with the substitution of a pole in place of the third barrel. The other two barrels each have a bucket that is three-quarters full of rabbit pellets placed on top. A flag is placed in one of these buckets. Riders may choose to run to the right or the left. They pick up the flag as they pass the first barrel, race past the pole, ride back to the second barrel, and attempt to place the flag in the second bucket. If the rider knocks over the first bucket or the pole, a five-second penalty is assessed. If the rider does not pick up

Barrel racing involves running around
three barrels in a certain pattern. Here
a horse and rider round one barrel.

the flag or misses the second bucket, no time is given. If the second bucket or barrel is knocked over, the rider is disqualified.

Again, most competitors wear jeans, boots, long-sleeved shirts, and hats. Your horse's tack can be basic, with a snaffle, a curb, or a hackamore bridle. You can use a saddle with a round skirt to enable your horse to use his loins without being rubbed or pinched by a longer square skirt.

KEYHOLE

In a keyhole race, horse and rider go across the starting line to a chalk box, stop, do a roll back, then race back to the finish line. This event rewards your horse's agility and speed. You are disqualified if you go outside the box.

A horse and rider participate in a keyhole race, in which you enter a chalk box, roll back, and run back out.

Most competitors wear jeans, boots, long-sleeved shirts, and hats. Your horse's tack can be basic, with a snaffle, a curb, or a hackamore bridle. You can use a saddle with a round skirt to enable your horse to use his loins without being rubbed or pinched by a longer square skirt.

POLE BENDING

In the most common pole-bending pattern, you race past a line of six poles spaced twenty-one feet apart. At the far end, you circle the pole and start weaving around each pole with a flying lead change between each one. At the end of the six poles, you circle and weave back down the row of poles, performing flying lead changes between the poles, then round the last one and race toward the finish line. You're allowed a running start, and you receive a five-second penalty for knocking down a pole. You are disqualified if you stray off course.

Most competitors wear jeans, boots, a long-sleeved shirt, and a hat. Your horse's tack can be basic, with a snaffle, a curb, or a hackamore bridle. You can use saddles with round skirts to enable your horse to use his loins without being rubbed or pinched by longer square skirts.

Cow Events

If your horse enjoys working with cattle, you can participate in several events, including cutting and roping, team penning, team sorting, and working cow horse, which showcases the versatility of the all-around cow horse and rider.

CUTTING

In a cutting competition, a panel of judges rates the performance of the horse-and-rider team as they demonstrate their cattle-handling skills. Each contestant is allowed 2½ minutes to cut at least two cows from the herd. The rider must bring at least one cow out from deep inside the herd during the allotted time (called a run). The rider can bring out a small group of cows, wait for all but one to go back to the herd, and select that cow. Or the rider can cut the other cow during the run from the edge of the herd. Extra credit is given if the rider drives the desired cow from deep inside the herd.

The contestant is assisted by four riders. Two are herd holders, positioned on either side of the herd to keep the cattle from drifting into the working area. Two turn-back riders stay between the cow being worked and the judge's stand; they turn the cow back to the contestant if it tries to escape to the far end of the working area.

When the rider has clearly separated one cow from the herd, the rider loosens his grip on the reins and allows the horse to have his head. The cow instinctively tries to return to the herd, and the horse does what he can to keep the cow away from the herd. Judges are looking for the horse's skill and style used to keep the cow under his control.

Your horse's quitting a cow or losing a cow, changing cows after you've committed to one, turning tail to a cow, and falling to the ground are all major penalties.

Cutting saddles have a flat seat that allows you to move with your horse. Riders often use split reins made of heavy harness leather. Although not required, most cutting riders wear chaps to increase their grip in the saddle.

Your horse will need splint boots for his front legs and back boots or skid boots for his hind legs. These boots will protect the horse's legs during the rigorous stops and turns demanded during a cutting competition.

ROPING

The two main categories are breakaway roping and team roping. In breakaway roping, the end of your rope is tied to your saddle horn with a piece of string. When the calf is released from the chute, you and your horse race after the calf, and you

In a working cow horse competition, you must cut one cow from inside the herd.

throw your loop completely over the calf's head. As the calf pulls away from you and your horse, the rope tightens and breaks away from the saddle horn where it's tied with the string.

In team roping, the steer is released from the chute and given a small head start. The header (the rider and horse pair that comes out of the start box first) comes up on the steer's left side, throws the loop and ropes the steer around the horns or neck. The header dallies the rope around the saddle horn and steers his or her horse to the left across the arena, pulling the steer behind them.

Next, the heeler (the rider and horse pair that comes out of the start box next) approaches the steer from behind and throws the loop so it catches both of the steer's hind feet. The heeler stops his or her horse while simultaneously dallying the rope around the saddle horn. When both ropers are successful, they turn their horses to face the steer and pull their ropes taut. A good roping team can do all this in less than ten seconds and often in less than five seconds.

Penalties can be assessed if the team begins chasing the steer before it has traveled the length of its allotted head start or if the heeler is only able to rope one hind foot. If either roper misses the steer, the team receives no score for the run.

Riders who rope are more concerned about function than fashion, so they typically wear long-sleeved shirts, hats, jeans, and boots. A stout roping saddle is the biggest requirement for any sort of roping activity. These saddles have extra-heavy-duty rigging and trees, and a rear cinch is a must.

TEAM PENNING

Evolving from the ranch work of separating cattle, today's team penning competitions have three-person teams that separate three specific cows from a herd of thirty. Each cow in the herd wears a number from 0 to 9, so three cows wear the same number.

When a number is called, the team must cut the three cows with the same number from the herd, keep them together, and herd them to a pen at the other end of the arena. The fastest team wins. Depending on the competitor's class, the team sorts and herds the cattle in sixty to ninety seconds.

As with most working events, contestants wear long-sleeved shirts, hats, jeans, and western boots. Some team penning competitions have dress codes that vary according to local custom, but most events do not.

TEAM SORTING

In team sorting, ten cows in a herd are numbered sequentially, 0 through 9. Teams of two or three riders are given numbers as they cross the start line. They sort and move the cattle in this order from the herd to a pen. So, if a team is given the number 4, they sort and move the cattle first with number 4 then 5, 6, 7, 8, 9, 0, 1, 2, and 3.

Team members must hold all the cattle except the cow being sorted behind the line or be disqualified. The objective is to sort each individual number, one at a time, without allowing the other cattle to cross the marked line. There is a ninety-second time limit.

Team sorters wear basic working clothing and use general tack.

WORKING COW HORSE

Working cow horse competitions, also known as "reined cow horse," combine cutting with reining. The best scores in three events decide the winner. The three events are herd work, reining, and fence work.

In herd work, you and your horse walk quietly into the herd and cut one cow. You work this cow side to side to show that you have the ability to keep it from returning to the herd. During your run of 2½ minutes, you can work up to three cows. Next, you run a reining pattern. These are the same patterns used by the NRHA (see "Reining" section on page 77).

Your final event is fence work, in which you cut one cow from the herd and demonstrate your ability to control the cow on the short

Fence work shows the horse and rider's ability to control the cow.

end of the arena from side to side. Then, you allow the cow to run down the long side of the arena against the fence. Next, you pass the cow, cut it off, and turn it around so it runs back down the fence toward its herd. You pass the cow and cut it off one more time, allow the cow to move into the center of the arena, then move it in a small circle in one direction and the other.

Working cow horse competitors generally wear basic work clothing, including jeans and chaps, hats, long-sleeved shirts, and boots.

Other Ways to Have Fun

If you're looking for even more ways to enjoy time with your horse, plenty of other options are available to choose from. American Quarter Horse Association-registered horses can enter Versatility Ranch Horse competitions, and any breed or type of horse can try competitive endurance riding, trail riding, games on horseback, cowboy mounted shooting, or ride and tie.

AQHA VERSATILITY RANCH HORSE

To showcase the all-around working ranch horse, the AQHA developed the Versatility Ranch Horse competition. It includes five categories: ranch riding, ranch trail, ranch cutting, working ranch horse, and ranch conformation. To be eligible for points, you and your horse must enter all five classes as a team.

In ranch riding, horses are shown at the walk, the jog, and the lope in both directions of the arena. Horses are also asked to change directions while on the rail, to stop, and to back. A horse is rewarded for traveling with his head held in a normal position, having his ears alert, and moving at a natural speed for the gait requested. The judges also look for smooth transitions between the gaits, for keeping the correct lead, and for maintaining the gait until the judge asks for a change. A rider must show his or her horse with only one hand on the reins, unless the horse is five years old or younger and is being shown in a snaffle bit or a hackamore (bosal).

In ranch trail, the course has a minimum of six obstacles and is designed to show a horse's ability and willingness to perform several tasks that might be asked of him during a normal day's ranch work. Mandatory obstacles include opening, passing through, and closing a gate; dragging a log either in a straight line or around a set pattern; and having the horse stand quietly while the rider dismounts, removes the bit completely from the horse's mouth and rebridles, and then picks up all four of the horse's feet. Optional obstacles include crossing a water hazard, being hobbled or ground tied, and crossing a bridge. The horse is judged on three gaits—walk, jog, and lope—performed between the obstacles.

In ranch cutting, you have 2½ minutes to cut a designated cow from a herd of at least ten, move it to the far end of the arena, and pen it there.

The working ranch horse class is judged in three sections—reining, cow work, and roping—illustrating the ranch horse's ability to rein, handle cattle, and put his rider in the position to rope and stop a cow. Scores from each section are combined for the final score of the class. Competing individually, you have a maximum of six minutes to complete the tasks.

In ranch conformation, horses are shown in a good working halter and judged on how well they represent the American Quarter Horse type. The sexes are shown together as one class. Horses are judged on their manners; how well they combine balance, structural correctness, and movement; whether they show adequate muscling; and how well they portray breed and sex characteristics. The ranch conformation class is held after the conclusion of the other four events.

For all five categories, a good working outfit is encouraged and should count more than silver-inlaid equipment. Silver on bridles and saddles is discouraged.

ENDURANCE RIDING

Endurance rides cover a measured course that must be ridden within a specified maximum time. Throughout the ride, there are mandatory rests for the horses. Your horse's health is checked by a veterinarian at certain checkpoints during the ride to ensure that he is sound and able to continue at each point. A horse is withdrawn from the ride if he is judged to be unsound or metabolically unfit.

At the end of the ride, the horse with the fastest time is the winner, provided that he is also judged by a veterinarian to be fit to continue.

Endurance rides vary in distance. Rides from 50 to 100 miles are covered in a single day. Rides that are longer than 100 miles are completed over a period of several days, with the horses typically covering 50 miles per day. Limited Distance rides offer shorter courses, ranging from between 25 and 35 miles.

Although endurance rides are technically races, with the fastest horse winning, many endurance riders participate with the goal of simply completing the ride, not winning the race. They compete for the sheer pleasure of spending hours with their horses.

Any well-fitting and comfortable saddle and bridle are acceptable for endurance riding, and riders wear clothing that is nonchafing and provides protection from the elements.

COMPETITIVE TRAIL RIDING

As with endurance riding, a competitive trail ride (CTR) covers a set, measured course, and your horse's health and well-being are closely monitored by a veterinarian. In CTR, however, you and your horse must ride within a window of time, but your elapsed time from start to finish is not a deciding factor in placement.

The biggest difference between CTR and endurance riding is that, in CTR, your horsemanship skills are judged in several different ways. First, judges make notes at checkpoints. Second, they observe you on the trail as you negotiate terrain and are asked to complete tasks such as mounting, backing, and side-passing. Finally, they evaluate your stabling area and campsite.

Your horse's condition, soundness, and overall health are evaluated by a veterinary judge during vet checks and on pulse and respiration stops throughout the ride. The veterinary judge will check the horse anywhere along the trail, and the horse is judged on whether his parameters have changed since the baseline established at the time your horse was checked in at the start of the race.

A horse and rider practice for an AQHA Versatility Ranch Horse competition.

Depending on your division, you will cover between thirty and sixty miles over two days, at speeds averaging between 3½ and 6 miles per hour. For the Novice division, rides are thirty to forty miles over two days, and the pace is a fast walk for most horses.

For competitive trail riding, you can ride in any saddle and bridle that you and your horse find comfortable. Many riders wear tights and other clothing specially made to avoid chafing for long hours in the saddle.

GAMES ON HORSEBACK

The games you can play just for fun on horseback are limited only by your imagination. Here are just a few.

Bun, Donut, or Marshmallow Race

Hotdog buns, donuts, or marshmallows are suspended from a high cross rail on strings. Riders race to the rail and eat the goody without using their hands. The first to eat the treat and gallop back to the start is the winner.

Musical Chairs

Rubber mats, cones, or other horse-safe markers are set up in a line, with one fewer than there are participants. The horses and riders circle the markers while the music plays; when the music stops, they race to a marker. The horse and rider left at the end of each round is excused from the game. The final horse and rider pair claiming the marker wins.

Egg and Spoon

Riders carry hardboiled eggs in spoons as they ride their horses and change gaits as requested by a judge. The last rider with the egg still in the spoon wins. This can also be played with a paper cup filled with water.

An endurance ride requires completing a course in a specified amount of time.

Trot or Consequences

Horses and riders first line up at the far end of the arena. When they are given the signal, the horses trot as fast as they can to the other end of the ring. The winner is the horse who comes in first without breaking into a lope. If a horse breaks into a lope, the rider has to turn his or her horse in a circle before continuing, thus losing time.

Bareback Dollar Ride

Bareback riders slip a dollar bill under one thigh, and no chaps are allowed! Riders follow the judge's cues to walk, jog, lope, stop, and change directions. The rider who keeps the dollar bill in place at the end of the class wins the dollar from each entrant.

Obstacle Race

The course can include a jump to cross, a barrel to crawl through, poles to bend around, and a sack race to the finish. The course combines both horse-and-human and human-only obstacles.

COWBOY MOUNTED SHOOTING

In cowboy mounted shooting, the rider shoots blank black-powder cartridges from .45-caliber pistols at ten helium balloons. The balloons can be arranged according to one of more than fifty possible patterns. Participants scored on accuracy and elapsed time.

During a typical event, you may ride three to six patterns. For example, one pattern may have five white balloons and five red balloons arranged either in a group or in a row. You may need to shoot all the white balloons first, then holster your first gun while finishing your run to the far end of the arena. Then you race back, shooting the red balloons with your second gun.

There's no danger involved with the shooting because the brass cartridge is loaded with black powder, and the cartridge is topped off with either ground corn cobs or ground walnut shells, instead of bullets. In addition, each event has a person responsible for loading the rider's guns as he or she enters the arena and a person responsible for unloading the guns after the rider is finished.

Any breed or type of horse is welcome in cowboy mounted shooting. The only requirement for your horse is that his temperament is quiet and steady through loud noises. And you'll need to do some training to accustom your horse to your shooting from the saddle, plus the quick turns and runs.

Most patterns are run in well under a minute. You receive penalties for each missed balloon, dropping your gun, going off course, and falling off your horse. Although speed is important, accuracy is usually the more important of the two factors.

Because it is based on life in the late 1800s, cowboy mounted shooting preserves the look and equipment of the era. You are required to dress in western attire. You can choose traditional western style, such a long-sleeve western shirt, five-pocket blue jeans covered by chinks or chaps, western boots, and a cowboy hat. Or you can dress to reflect the period by wearing, for example, a shirt without a collar, high-waist pants with buttons (not zippers), and an old-style cowboy hat. Mounted cowboy shooters use .45-caliber single-action revolvers like those used in the late 1800s.

RIDE AND TIE

Ride and tie consists of a three-member team composed of two people and one horse. All three begin at the starting gun, with one person riding and the other person running. The horse-and-rider pair go a predetermined distance, where the rider stops and securely ties the horse. The rider then continues on foot while the horse waits for the second person to catch up. When the runner reaches the equine teammate, he or she mounts and rides to the next point. The team continues leapfrogging riders this way until the end of the ride.

Of course, the fitter the people are, the faster they will travel on the ground and the higher the team will place in the rankings. However, walking is perfectly acceptable, and even the fittest competitors walk at times because the courses are usually chosen for their difficulty (mountains, altitude, rocky trail, and so on).

Ride-and-tie courses are generally designed in a series of loops that keep coming back to a central point for each veterinary check. Because the loops are not usually more than fifteen miles in length, horses and riders don't need to carry much equipment other than water (for the riders) and perhaps a boot (for the horse, in case he loses a shoe).

This is a timed event, and all the team's members must cross the finish line, though not at the same time. As in endurance riding, the equine team member must pass a veterinary check. If a team's horse is not fit to continue, that team is disqualified.

In addition to a safe and easy-to-use tie rope, the only piece of specialized equipment needed by some teams is a set of double stirrups. These stirrups have two different areas for your feet in case you and your partner have very different leg lengths. The style of saddle doesn't matter, as long as your horse finds it comfortable. Many ride-and-tie participants use wool saddle covers, especially if they ride in running shorts.

CHAPTER 6

Conclusion

*l*ike any worthwhile endeavor in life, becoming the best western rider you can be is a never-ending journey of discovery.

As you continue to challenge yourself, remember that your progress may not always be in a straight line. There may be times when you make huge advances quickly, but you also may go through times when you feel that everything's a struggle and that you're actually losing ground. Hang in there and don't despair.

If you can embrace the times when you struggle and see them as a necessary part of learning, you can actually begin to treasure these times and know they will get you further along the journey. It takes faith, but keep riding, keep an open mind, and keep doing your best. Believe that your horse is doing her best, too. If you stay on the path you're on, more often than not, you'll see big improvements after one of these difficult phases. They are just that: phases. They will pass.

As you've seen, this book is a coaching guide to help you develop into the best advanced western rider you can be. Rather than presenting cookie-cutter solutions to common riding questions, it challenges you to search for and discover answers from within yourself on your own. There is no blueprint for becoming an advanced rider, nor a single way to get from here to there. However, all the answers you need are within you. What you achieve is limited only by your imagination and your belief in yourself and your horse. So start today. Try, explore, innovate. Your journey is just beginning. Have fun and remember to enjoy the ride!

Abaco Barb Wild Horse Fund
2829 Bird Ave.
Suite 5
PMB #170
Miami, FL 33133
www.arkwild.org

**American Bashkir
Curly Registry**
857 Beaver Road
Walton, KY 41094
www.abcregistry.org

**American Connemara
Pony Society**
P.O. Box 100
Middlebrook, VA 24459
www.acps.org

**American Endurance
Ride Conference**
P.O. Box 6027
Auburn, CA 95604
866-271-AERC (2372)
www.aerc.org

The American Hanoverian Society
4067 Iron Works Parkway
Suite 1
Lexington, KY 40511
859-255-4141
www.hanoverian.org

**American Holsteiner
Horse Association**
222 E. Main St., # 1
Georgetown, KY 40324
502-863-4239
www.holsteiner.com

American Horse Council
1616 H St. N.W., 7th Floor
Washington, D.C. 20006
202-296-4031
www.horsecouncil.org

American Indian Horse Registry
9028 State Park Road
Lockhart, TX 78644
512-398-6642
www.indianhorse.com

**American Morgan
Horse Association**
122 Bostwick Road
Shelburne, VT 05482
802-985-4944
www.morganhorse.com

**American Mustang
and Burro Association**
P.O. Box 608
Greenwood, DE 19950
www.ambainc.com

**American Paint
Horse Association**
P.O. Box 961023
Fort Worth, TX 76161
817-834-APHA (2742)
www.apha.com

**American Quarter
Horse Association**
P.O. Box 200
Amarillo, TX 79168
806-376-4811
www.aqha.com

**American Riding
Instructors Association**
28801 Trenton Court
Bonita Springs, FL 34134
239-948-3232
www.riding-instructor.com

**American Saddlebred
Horse Association**
4083 Iron Works Parkway
Lexington, KY 40511
859-259-2742
www.asha.net

American Trails
P.O. Box 491797
Redding, CA 96049
530-547-2060
www.americantrails.org

American Trakehner Association
1536 W. Church St.
Newark, OH 43055
www.americantrakehner.com

American Warmblood Society
2 Buffalo Run Road
Center Ridge, AR 72027
501-893-2777
www.americanwarmblood.org

American Youth Horse Council
6660 #D-451 Delmonico
Colorado Springs, CO 80919
800-TRY-AYHC (879-2942)
www.ayhc.com

Appaloosa Horse Club Inc.
2720 W. Pullman Road
Moscow, ID 83843
208-882-5578
www.appaloosa.com

**Arabian Horse
Registration of America**
10805 E. Bethany Drive
Aurora, CO 80014
303-696-4500
www.arabianhorses.org

**Certified Horsemanship
Association**
4037 Iron Works Parkway, Suite 180
Lexington, KY 40511
800-724-1446
www.cha-ahse.org

**Cowboy Mounted
Shooting Association**
P.O. Box 1529
Columbia, TN 38402
888-960-0003
www.cowboymountedshooting.com

Curly Sporthorse International
P.O. Box 129
Cross Anchor, SC 29331
864-316-4672
www.curlysporthorse.org

**International Andalusian
& Lusitano Horse Association**
101 Carnoustie N., Box 200
Birmingham, AL 35242
205-995-8900
www.ialha.org

**International
Curly Horse
Organization**
HC31 Box 102A
Williamsburg, NM 87942
575-740-4159
www.curlyhorses.org

**Kiger Mesteño
Association**
11124 N.E. Halsey
Suite 591
Portland, OR 97220
www.kigermustangs.org

**National Cutting
Horse Association**
260 Bailey Ave.
Fort Worth, TX 76107
817-244-6188
www.nchacutting.com

**National High School
Rodeo Association Inc.**
12001 Tejon St.
Suite 128
Denver, CO 80234
303-452-0820
www.nhsra.org

**National Professional
Rodeo Association**
P.O. Box 212
Mandan, ND 58554
701-663-4973
www.npra.com

**National Reined
Cow Horse Association**
13181 U.S. Highway 177
Byars, OK 74831
580-759-4949
www.nrcha.com

**National Reining
Horse Association**
3000 N.W. 10th St.
Oklahoma City, OK 73107
405-946-7400
www.nrha.com

**The Nokota
Horse Conservancy**
208 N.W. First St.
Linton, ND 58552
701-254-4302
www.nokota.org

**North American Riding
for the Handicapped
Association**
P.O. Box 33150
Denver, CO 80233
800-369-RIDE (7433)
www.narha.org

**North American
Trail Ride Conference**
P.O. Box 224
Sedalia, CO 80135
303-688-1677
www.natrc.org

**Palomino Horse
Breeders of America**
15253 E. Skelly Drive
Tulsa, OK 74116
918-438-1234
www.palominohba.com

**Performance
Horse Registry**
U.S. Equestrian Federation
4047 Iron Works Parkway
Lexington, KY 40511
859-258-2472
www.phr.com

Rails-to-Trails Conservancy
The Duke Ellington Building
2121 Ward Court N.W.
5th Floor
Washington, D.C. 20037
202-331-9696
www.railtrails.org

**The Ride and Tie
Association**
8215 E. White Oak Ridge, #41
Orange, CA 92869
www.rideandtie.org

**Southwest Spanish
Mustang Association**
P.O. Box 948
Antlers, OK 74523
580-326-8069
www.southwestspanishmustang
  association.com

**Spanish Barb
Breeders Association**
P.O. Box 1628
Silver City, NM 88062
www.spanishbarb.com

Spanish Mustang Registry
323 County Road 419
Chilton, TX 76632
254-546-2177
www.spanishmustang.org

**Swedish Warmblood
Association
of North America**
P.O. Box 788
Socorro, NM 87801
505-835-1318
www.swanaoffice.org

**Tennessee Walking
Horse Breeders' and
Exhibitors' Association**
P.O. Box 286
Lewisburg, TN 37091
931-359-1574
www.twhbea.com

**United States
Equestrian Federation**
4047 Iron Works Parkway
Lexington, KY 40511
859-258-2472
www.usef.org

**United States Mounted
Games Association**
5400 Old Sligo Road
LaGrange, KY 40031
502-222 4016
www.usmga.us

**United States Team
Penning Association**
P.O. Box 4170
Fort Worth, TX 76164
817-378-8082
www.ustpa.com

**United States Team
Roping Championships**
P.O. Box 1198
Stephenville, TX 76401
254-968-0002
www.ustrc.com

**Women's Professional
Rodeo Association**
1235 Lake Plaza Drive
Suite 127
Colorado Springs, CO 80906
719-576-0900
www.wpra.com

aids: the communication signals given by a rider to his or her horse, which can be given by external equipment or by the rider's body. See also "artificial aids" and "natural aids."

Alexander technique: a method that works to change movement habits; improve freedom of movement, balance, and coordination; and release unnecessary tension to allow the body to move with greater ease and efficiency.

artificial aids: items such as a whip, a crop, or a spur

bar: the toothless, bony space in the horse's mouth where the bit lies, located between the incisors and the molars; also, the two pieces of a saddle tree that span the horse's back parallel to the spine. (The bars are connected to the cantle in the rear and to the swells in the front of the saddle.)

barrel: the area of a horse's body between the forelegs and the hind legs, where the ribs are located

bitless bridle: any sort of bridle that does not use a bit in the horse's mouth, including a bosal, a hackamore, a mechanical hackamore, and a sidepull

bosal: a type of bitless bridle with a simple noseband usually made of braided rawhide and knotted under the horse's chin, with the reins attached to the knot

brace: to use more muscle, power, or energy than is necessary to complete a task; also, a part on a spade bit connecting the port to the cheek

breastplate: a device used across the horse's chest that attaches to the saddle to prevent it from slipping; also known as a "breast collar"

bridle: headgear used to guide a horse when riding or driving; the entire headgear assembly including headstall, bit, and reins

canter: a three-beat gait. It has the same footfalls as the western lope.

chaps: leggings, usually made of leather, worn over jeans or trousers. They offer extra grip in the saddle and protection against shrubs and brush when trail riding. They are often worn by riders in the show ring.

cinch: the western term for "girth," which is a band that goes under the horse's belly and keeps the saddle on the horse's back

collection: a natural movement when a horse coils like a spring

combination bit: any bit that uses leverage with shanks and lip pressure, as well as a jointed mouthpiece

counter canter: taking the lead contrary to the direction of travel. It is different from being on the wrong lead, as the horse still needs to be bent in the direction of the leading leg.

crop: a short riding whip with a looped lash

cross training: working the horse in more than one discipline, such as trail riding, showing, cattle work, and dressage. Cross training helps the horse gain more athletic ability and additional skills, and it benefits the horse physically because he is not overusing any single part of his body by doing only one discipline.

cue: a signal from the rider that requests the horse to respond with a certain movement. The signal can be a natural aid or an artificial aid. See also "artificial aids" and "natural aids."

curb bit: a bit that works based on leverage in the horse's mouth, regardless of the shape or configuration of the mouthpiece. It has shanks of varying lengths, and it creates pressure on the bars of the horse's mouth and sometimes on the roof of the horse's mouth.

dally: to wind the rope around the saddle horn after a cow has been roped. The friction helps secure the rope to the saddle horn rather than having to tie the rope.

deaden: to desensitize a horse's mouth or sides by using the bit or leg aids excessively and without clarity

diagonal: the movement of a foreleg in unison with the opposite hind leg. At the jog, the left front and right hind legs move together in a diagonal, and vice versa.

direct rein: using a rein to pull the horse's head in the direction the rider requests. See also "indirect rein."

Feldenkrais: named after Moshe Feldenkrais, this method uses movement to increase a person's body awareness. Through awareness, one is able to improve one's flexibility, posture, and breathing.

flying lead change: in the lope, the horse changes from one lead to the other in midair instead of transitioning with steps of a jog or a walk. See also "lead."

footfall: the order in which the horse's feet leave and come into contact with the ground. Footfall changes depending on which gait the horse is in.

gullet: the space under the saddle that spans the horse's spine. There should be no pressure on the horse's spine along the gullet, and the bars of the tree should rest sufficiently away from the spine rather than right next to it.

gymkhana games: informal speed games, contests, and races on horseback

hackamore: a type of bitless bridle with a noseband, usually made of braided rawhide, that applies pressure on the nose instead of using a bit for guidance and signaling

headstall: the pieces of a bridle not including the bit and the reins. The headstall includes the cheek pieces, the throatlatch, the browband, and the noseband, if used.

horn: the raised part in front of a western saddle. It is often used to dally the rope when working with cattle.

indirect rein (neck rein): laying the rein against the horse's neck so the horse turns only from the pressure of the rein, not from contact with the bit or bosal. See also "direct rein."

jog: a two-beat diagonal gait, which has the same footfall as the trot. When the horse is jogging, the right front leg and the left hind leg move together as a pair, and the left front leg and the right hind leg move together as a pair.

jumping hackamore: leather noseband or leather-covered rope noseband with two rings attached near the mouth of the horse

lasso: a thirty- to forty-foot rope with a running noose for roping cattle and horses

lateral work: sideways movement, varying from being completely sideways in the sidepass to maintaining sideways movement while going forward in the leg yield

latigo: a long piece of leather or nylon that is used to tighten the cinch around the horse's belly

lead: the foreleg that takes the longer stride while the horse is at the lope or canter indicates which lead he is on. A horse is on the left lead if the left leg reaches farther in the lope or canter, and he is on the right lead when the right leg reaches farther in the lope or canter. When the horse is traveling clockwise, he will be on the right lead, and vice versa. See also "counter canter."

leg yield: the horse moves forward and sideways at the same time, crossing the forelegs and hind legs to the front. See also "lateral work."

longe (or lunge): working a horse on a long line, usually with a long whip used as an extension of the hand, and with the handler standing in the middle of the pen

loose rein: reins that hang loosely without any pulling or contact between the rider's hands and the horse's mouth

lope: a three-beat gait with the same footfall as the canter. If the horse is on the left lead, the footfall is right hind, left hind and right front landing together, then left front. See also "lead."

mecate: a single length of horsehair rein or rope about 22 feet long that is tied to the hackamore knot, looped to create reins, with the remaining length used as an attached rope

mechanical hackamore: a bitless bridle that has long metal shanks and a curb chain, making its action similar to the leverage action of a curb bit

natural aids: hands, seat, leg, voice, weight, mind, intention, focus, center, energy

neck reining: guiding a horse using just the weight of the rein on the horse's neck rather than with pressure from the bit, the hackamore, or the bosal

pelham bit: a leverage bit with short shanks and two sets of rings to attach double reins

post: to rise and sit in time with the rhythm of the horse's trot

rein hand: the hand that holds the reins. Traditionally, the rein hand is the left hand so the right hand can be used for roping, opening gates, and so on.

romal reins: reins that join to form a single long lash or whip with a leather popper on the end.

roping: lassoing cattle with a long rope, either around their heads, horns, or hind legs while on horseback. See also "dally."

scapula: the proper name for the horse's shoulder blade

self-carriage: the horse's and the human's body posture that is balanced, correctly aligned biomechanically, without reliance on bracing or unnecessary muscular tension

sidepull: usually a lariat noseband, knotted at the sides of the horse's head to rings where the reins attach

snaffle bit: a nonleverage bit that applies pressure to the corners of the horse's mouth and tongue. It can have a broken or a solid mouthpiece.

spade bit: a complex bit that has a high spoon port, braces, a roller, and shanks

split reins: reins that are not joined or attached and that can be held in two hands or in one hand

spur: usually a round rowel that attaches to the rider's boot heel and is used as an aid in addition to the leg

tack: all the gear used to ride or handle a horse, including a halter, a lead rope, a saddle, a pad, and a bridle

tie down: a strap (or self-contained) piece of tack that connects the noseband to the breastplate and prevents the horse from raising her head past a certain point

tree: the wooden or plastic framework on which a saddle is built

walk: a four-beat gait in which the horse's feet move together on the same side; for example: right hind, right front, left hind, left front

withers: the highest point of the horse's back where the neck and back join